IF YOU TAKE MY MEANING

Theory into Practice in Human Communication

IF YOU TAKE
MY MEANING

Theory into Practice in
Human Communication

Richard Ellis and Ann McClintock
Lecturers in Communication, The Queen's College,
Glasgow

Edward Arnold
A division of Hodder & Stoughton
LONDON NEW YORK MELBOURNE AUCKLAND

© 1990 Richard Ellis and Ann McClintock

First published in Great Britain 1990

Distributed in the USA by Routledge, Chapman and Hall, Inc.
29 West 35th Street, New York, NY 10001

British Library Cataloguing in Publication Data

Ellis, Richard
   If you take my meaning: theory into practice in human
   communication.
   1. Man. Communication
   I. Title   II. McClintock, Ann
   302.2

   ISBN 0-7131-6620-7

Typeset in 10/11pt Century Schoolbook by
Colset Private Limited, Singapore
Printed and bound in Great Britain by Biddles Ltd, Guildford &
King's Lynn for Edward Arnold, a division of Hodder and
Stoughton Limited, Mill Road,
Dunton Green, Sevenoaks, Kent TN13 2YA

CONTENTS

ACKNOWLEDGEMENTS

The authors would like to thank the following for their help in the preparation of this text.

Nan Kelly and Orna Mulrooney, students of The Queen's College, Glasgow who read over parts of the text and provided valuable comment; colleagues and students at the above college; Konrad Hopkins for his advice in preparation of the text; Lesley Riddle, Senior Editor, Edward Arnold for her help throughout and to members of our families for their help and forbearance: Andy, Carol, Grace, Charles and Victoria.

The publishers would like to thank the following for permission to reproduce material in this volume:

The proprietor of the Nescafé and Gold Blend Trade Marks (The Nestlé Company Ltd) for the advertisement Illustration B; Tipp-Ex Ltd for the advertisement Illustration C.

Every effort has been made to trace and acknowledge ownership of copyright. The publishers will be glad to make suitable arrangements with any copyright holders whom it has not been possible to contact.

INTRODUCTION

In writing this book the authors started with two basic premises. First, that competence in communication is advantageous in virtually every sphere of human activity. Secondly, that competence requires both a knowledge and understanding of theory and the skill to apply the theory effectively and appropriately in a range of diverse situations.

Therefore, this book is not simply an account of communication theory. Nor is it an instruction manual outlining procedures to be adopted in specific situations. Rather, it represents an attempt to produce an interactive text which will encourage our readers to become actively involved in developing competence.

We have aimed the book primarily at students in further and higher education taking courses in Communication Studies, and at those other undergraduates who, in their main course, are taking a Behavioural/Social Science component which includes Communication. We hope that students will find the text relevant and useful in providing a clear introduction to many of the topic areas and theories they will meet in their studies.

The experimental research which has enabled the fomulation of communication theory has been carried out in a wide range of disciplines, from psychology and sociology to linguistics, phonetics and many others. The book brings together a number of the more important theories from the various disciplines and shows how they have increased our knowledge and understanding of the human communication process. It invites readers to apply the theories in order to test their validity and achieve a personal understanding of what they mean in practice. And it suggests a range of exercises whereby practical communication skills may be developed.

The Exercises

Each chapter includes a number of exercises, which can be done either by an individual working alone or by two or more people working as a group. Some require the use of readily available equipment such as a tape recorder, TV or radio, magazines and newspapers. In a few cases access to a video camera is desirable but not essential.

The exercises range from simple checklists which readers can use to test how far their own experiences accord with the predictions outlined in the theory, to more complex games, role-plays or experiments which not only test the validity of the theory but provide practice for the development of skill. In some cases it is left to our readers to make deductions or inferences about the theory on the basis of experimentation with the activities suggested.

A number of the exercises raise many more questions than it is possible to answer within the scope of this book. The references or follow-up texts suggested at the end of each chapter should enable readers to discover some of the answers. In many cases, however, there are no neat, hard and fast solutions to the exercises, simply a forum for fascinating speculation.

Exercises are highlighted in bold text. Definitions and key concepts are in italics to emphasize their importance. Readers who decide to 'dip into' specific chapters, rather than working through the book from the start, will find cross-references, which should enable them to pick up on key concepts which have been dealt with in earlier chapters but which have relevance to the subject of the chapter they are reading. Most chapters also contain a summary of the main points. All include a list of references to enable interested readers to pursue specific aspects of communication in more depth.

The Theories

The first chapter draws on psychological theories which show how the processes of individual perception affect the ways in which each of us takes in information about ourselves, our environment and the other people in it. The information we take in leads to the development of a set of attitudes and values.

Chapter Two explains some of the ways in which attitudes and values affect how we communicate, who we choose to communicate with and the manner we adopt when doing so.

Personal attitudes also influence the extent to which we are prepared to listen to what others have to say, what we remember, and the interpretation we place on what we have heard. Chapter Three draws on some of the linguistic research which demonstrates this relationship.

Chapter Four also examines this relationship in the context of non-verbal communication – body-language, gesture, pace, pitch, emphasis and other features which affect how we express ourselves, how others react to us, and how we, in turn, read meaning into the non-verbal signals given by others.

The question of meaning is further explored in Chapter Five. This chapter looks in some detail at the ways in which theorists have attempted to model two distinct ways of explaining communication. One set of theorists sees communication as a process which involves the deliberate transmission and reception of messages, and is primarily concerned with how this process can be improved to ensure that messages sent will be received with the minimum of distortion. A contrasting approach is provided by those linguists and philosophers who are less concerned with the transmission process, and more interested in how meaning is ascribed to the messages themselves. The ways in which language both affects and is affected by the culture in which it is used is an important element in determining how individuals interpret meaning.

Cultural factors can also affect an individual's self-image and role behaviour. Chapter Six shows some of the ways in which perception of role behaviour may be coloured by stereotyped cultural attitudes which may create role-conflict and difficulties in communication with others.

Communication with others in groups and organizations is the subject of the two following chapters. Chapter Seven takes a sociological perspective and examines the formation of human groups and the dynamic interactions which occur between individuals in their communication as members of specific groups. Chapter Eight takes this one stage further and analyses the relationship between the individual, the group and the organization. It outlines some of the methods which have been employed to enable communication to take place both within and between organizations, and it highlights some of the recent advances in technology which have had an impact on organizational communication.

Chapter Nine deals with a particular aspect of organizational communication – the interviews between individuals which determine whether they are selected for membership of an organization, how their performance is appraised as a member, and the kind of techniques which may be employed in giving guidance and counselling to those who require help or advice.

The final chapter goes beyond individual or group communication to look at some of the ways in which the mass media of communication may be used to inform and influence people through the use of prepared presentation, carefully planned rhetoric or persuasive style.

These theories have been selected because we believe they provide an overview of the progression of the communication process from its beginnings in self-awareness to its skilled expression in public presentation. They are by no means the only theories which could have been included, nor have we attempted to provide an in-depth analysis. That would require a book of much greater length and complexity.

We have had to select very carefully and have omitted many theories and approaches, especially those relating to the oral and written skills of communication. These have been the subject of a number of texts in recent years. Our treatment of the mass media has also had to be limited – again this would have required a textbook to itself in order to deal adequately with the many theories that have gained currency in this area.

What we hope our selection has achieved is a simple, readable introduction which will stimulate interest in the subject of communication, encourage active experimentation, and provide a foundation for further study and the development of skill.

CHAPTER ONE
PERCEPTION

Imagine you are a woman walking through a crowded city centre store. You see in the distance someone whom you vaguely recognize. As you move closer the person begins to look more familiar. She obviously thinks she knows you too because she's looking towards you in a rather puzzled way. Suddenly you realize why. You are looking at your own reflection!

It may seem ludicrous that people could look at their own reflection and not recognize themselves instantly. And yet many will admit to having had this sort of experience at least a couple of times in their lives.

Can you suggest any reasons why it should be possible for us to fail to recognize something which is usually so easily recognizable as our own face and body?

Some possible reasons might be the fact that you are in an unfamiliar setting and don't expect to see your own reflection; or you might be concentrating on something else; or you may have developed a mental picture of what you look like which, at first, doesn't correspond to the image you see in front of you; or you may have been fooled by the illusion created by the mirror and find it illogical to accept that you can be seeing yourself. Whatever the particular reason on any occasion, what has been experienced is a failure in perception.

In this chapter we look at human perception and the various ways in which it affects communication. So let's start first of all by giving a broad definition of what we mean by perception.

Perception may be regarded as information which is taken in by the senses, processed by the brain, stored in memory and produces some form of physical or mental response.

Sensory Information

We know that human beings are equipped with the five senses of taste, touch, smell, sight and hearing. It is through the interaction of the environment with these senses that we gain information about ourselves and the world we live in. If any one of these senses is impaired it is correspondingly more difficult to learn.

The child who is born deaf and blind, for example, will be unaware of the spoken word and will have great difficulty in establishing any form of satisfactory communication in his early years. The child may have the potential to develop normal, or even above average intelligence, but his inability to take in information through two of his major senses will be a considerable barrier to his ever being able fully to realize that potential.

But even among those who have no sensory handicap there will be some differences in the normal functioning of the five senses. Some people with average hearing ability may have very good eyesight, or a strong sense of smell, or a poorer than average ability to discriminate by touch alone. There can, in fact, be quite wide variations between the abilities of people who would still be considered to have normal sensory functioning. Research has shown, however, that there are well defined limits to normal functioning (Gilling & Brightwell, 1982).

We know that human beings can hear sounds only within a fairly limited frequency range, can see only a limited intensity of light, respond only to a limited range of taste sensations and are unaware of smells or touch sensations which are very faint. Psychologists refer to the boundaries of human senses as *absolute sense thresholds*.

> **Blindfold a number of friends and note how accurately each is able to identify a number of different household products –**
>
> > **by smell alone**
> > **by taste only**
> > **by touch.**
>
> **See how quickly each responds to a faint sound like a pin or a paperclip being dropped on a carpeted surface.**
> **Note whether any individual seemed to have all his or her senses sharper than the others or whether ability varied across the senses in the same individual.**

Although human beings can perceive only those sensations which lie within the normal range of sense thresholds, they have been able to discover that other species respond to a different range of stimuli. This in turn has made it possible for man to develop tools such as X-ray machines and radios which allow him to make use of light or sound waves which he cannot perceive using his own senses.

> **Can you think of any other examples of discoveries which have allowed human beings to make use of sensory stimuli which they are unable to perceive through their normal senses?**
> **Can you suggest reasons why man, with his limited sensory perception, has been able to make these discoveries?**

Brain Processes

It would be possible to put forward quite a number of reasons in answer to the last question, but probably the most common answer would centre around our ability to use our brains. The sense organs could be likened to receivers which are tuned to receive information, while the brain might be regarded as the control mechanism which makes the information meaningful.

We know, for example, that when we look at something the image on the retina of the eye is actually upside down. It is the brain which processes the image and enables us to see things the right way up. Similarly, when we see a car in the distance the effect of perspective makes it look very small. We actually see it as small, but because we have learned to correct for the effects of perspective we perceive it to be a car of normal size and therefore reason that it must be a distance away.

Piaget and other child psychologists have demonstrated that from childhood onwards we are constantly learning how to interpret the information we obtain from our senses. A long thin roll of plasticine may look as if it should weigh more than a small, tightly packed ball of the same substance. If, however, we have previously weighed the two and know them to be the same weight, then – as adults – we will disregard what our eyes are telling us and trust in our reasoning that weight stays the same no matter what shape it takes! Children under the age of seven or so may be less able to trust their reasoning powers and may be more inclined to trust the evidence of their eyes (Piaget & Inhelder, 1958).

Similarly, children may attend to every new sound they hear and be acutely aware of sounds around them. As adults we have learned to screen out a lot of the noise around us and to be aware only of hearing what we are attending to at the time. Adults have also learned that something which tastes and smells awful may be safe to swallow and may even be good medicine! Part of the process of brain development, therefore, seems to lie in learning not only how to interpret the information we obtain from our eyes, ears and other senses, but when to disregard the sensory information and trust in our powers of reasoning (Gregory, 1977).

Look at the two lines below. Which appears longer?

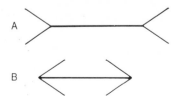

Fig 1.1   The Muller–Lyer Illusion

If you've never seen this figure before you would probably believe on the evidence of your eyes that line A was longer than line B. Those who have seen it before will probably know that the two lines are the same length. While the sceptics will no doubt measure them just to be completely sure!

A similar effect can be seen in the figure below.

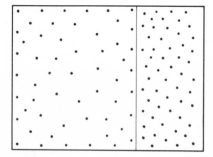

Fig 1.2

At first glance it looks as if there are more dots on the right side than on the left. In fact there are the same number on each side but those on the right are packed into a smaller space. British Rail used this device in one of their advertising campaigns, with a slogan which suggested that the dots on the left were the trains that ran late, the dots on the right those which ran to time. In this case there were more dots on the right side, but not many more. Some travellers complained that the advert was intended to mislead and British Rail were asked to remove the advert by the Advertising Standards Authority – the body that oversees advertising and tries to ensure that adverts do not mislead the public.

> **Can you think of occasions in your own life where you have accepted the evidence of your senses and found that you were wrong?**

Storing in Memory

Learning to discount or reinterpret the information we obtain from our senses is a part of the learning process. Another part of this process, and one which we will refer to a number of times within this book, is the human ability to make comparisons, to discriminate, to label and to categorize.

The information we take in via our senses may be vague and ambiguous. For example, we perceive a round red object. The information we have already stored in memory allows us to identify the object more precisely and to label it as an apple, a cherry, a ball or whatever. In order to do this we depend on the brain's capacity to store information. By comparing new sensory information with information already stored in memory we can arrive at a whole variety of conclusions ranging from simple statements like 'that is red and not green' to highly complex statements such as 'the sum on the square of the hypotenuse of a right-angled triangle is equal to the sum of the squares on the two adjacent sides'!

Expectancy Sets

Precisely because human beings have such strong reasoning abilities, and because part of that reasoning is, from our earliest years, devoted to learning when to accept or reject the evidence of our senses, we arrive at a stage where we have learned what information to expect from our senses. We assume that a glowing red cooker element will be hot and we know not to touch it. We are capable of very fine judgement as to whether we will be able to drive our car through a narrow gateway. And even though we can't smell garlic on our own breath we assume, from past experience, that other people will.

Obviously this ability allows us to take sensible action to ensure our own safety. It also enables us to make scientific predictions and judgements on phenomena which we have noticed in the natural world. We soon learn, for example, that when dark clouds mass in the sky there is a strong possibility that rain will follow!

However, perceptual ability which allows us to function so effectively in these ways can sometimes be a hindrance to us in relating to and communicating with other people. For example, if we have learned to dislike someone we will have built up a number of expectations about how we will relate to and communicate with that person, and we might well be inclined to discount or ignore what they say.

> **Jot down a situation in which you might have to communicate with someone whom you dislike.**
>
> **Suggest what might happen to the communication flow between you when you are the speaker or the listener.**

Your suggestions may well have included some of the following:

> it is difficult to listen to someone you dislike;
> it is difficult to sustain an easy flow of communication;
> it may be difficult to remember accurately what the other person said;
> it may be particularly easy to remember what was said because it was so predictable;

the language used was more restrained and polite than with someone you like;
the language used was less restrained and polite!

We will be analysing these and other communication difficulties more fully in later chapters. What we can say here is that we perceive information differently depending on whether we expect it to be favourable or unfavourable to us. If someone who likes you says 'well done' you tend to accept the words at their face value. Hearing the same words from someone who we think dislikes us we are likely to discount the words themselves and to 'hear' sarcasm or feel that the other person is being patronizing, hypocritical or simply untruthful.

What we have been told about others can also affect our perceptions. For example, a new lecturer was introduced to two groups of students. The factual details given to both groups were the same, but to the first group the lecturer was described as a rather warm, friendly person, while the second group was told he was rather cold and distant. When later asked to assess the lecture the students assessments reflected this bias. In addition, those who had been told he was cold actually participated less in the lesson (Kelly, 1950).

In another study people were asked to rate applicants on their suitability for a job. In each case the information given was the same except for the gender attributed to the candidate. When asked to explain the reasons why they rated candidates as they did it became clear that knowing the gender of the individual altered the raters' perceptions of the information given (Naylor *et al.*, 1980). It is all too easy to 'see' something which favours our opinion. It is equally easy to avoid seeing something which may go against our viewpoint.

Working in a group of about four select a topic on which there are a number of contrasting viewpoints.

Prepare your own contribution carefully.

The first person in the group makes his or her point; the second person summarizes that point and then adds his own contribution; this process continues until the last person in the group who has the tricky task of summarizing all the previous points before adding his own.

As the points are being circulated and summarized keep a very close eye on your particular ones and see what happens to them.

At the end of the round find out which points were maintained all through and which were lost in the summarizing.

Try to discover why some points were lost. You may discover that these were the ones which the next speaker disagreed with or considered to be unimportant.

You might like to make use of a tape recorder to check on the extent of distortion which occurs in this process.

Some early experiments by Bartlett (1932) into recall of complex events showed quite dramatically how listeners alter remembered material to suit their view of the world. Bartlett varied the time intervals and was thus able to isolate the effects of increased time lapse on how well the material was remembered. Some rather interesting changes occurred when subjects were asked to reconstruct the story. Some of the unusual elements were 'levelled down' and made less unusual. Others were 'sharpened up' or made even stranger. Bartlett concluded that some people like to 'see' the world as regular. These are the levellers. The sharpeners like to accentuate differences and see the world as more complex and variable.

More recent work by management theorists has shown that people tend to view other people according to their own preferred view. Someone who likes to be friendly may judge others primarily on this quality without noticing other aspects of their personality or behaviour. An authoritarian manager could react more favourably to a subordinate who also displays authoritarian tendencies, while a manager who prefers a democratic style of interaction might give a more favourable rating to a junior who is less deferential and more relaxed (Zalkind & Costello, 1962; Mitchell & Larson, 1987).

Subliminal Perception

In the examples above there is an assumption that disliking someone – or being disliked – is part of a normal rational process, or is a response to a particular expectancy set which distorts our perception. Sometimes, however, we experience a strong feeling of liking or disliking for someone the very first time we meet and before we have been told what to expect. In analysing the feeling we can find no rational explanation for it.

Psychologists have suggested that one possible reason for this instant reaction is that we are either attracted to or repelled by the other person's body odour. Not the body odours we are aware of and disguise by means of deodorants, etc., but a much fainter odour which we cannot detect at the conscious level but which is capable of being picked up by our sense of smell and processed by the brain (Krames *et al.*, 1974). Our subsequent feeling is a direct response to this processing.

Moreover, when we are attracted to someone the pupils in our eyes dilate. Without realizing it we may start to feel attracted to someone because the pupils of their eyes are telling us that they find us attractive (Aronson, 1972).

Stimuli like these, which are either very brief or so faint as to lie at the very extreme limits of the human sense thresholds, have been called *subliminal* – literally just below the level of conscious perception but not outiside the level of reception by the sense organs. We perceive, but we are unaware that we have done so.

It has never actually been proved, but it has been claimed that advertisers have made use of this phenomenon in trying to persuade us to buy their product. For example, an American soft drinks company is reputed to have flashed the name of their product on to the screen a number of times during the showing of a film. The name was exposed on the screen for such a brief period that the audience did not notice it at the conscious level but when it came to the interval the sales of that particular product were reported to have risen dramatically (Dixon, 1971). As a result of this case, the US advertising authorities stepped in and placed a ban on subliminal advertising since, if it worked as the advertisers claimed, it seemed to put the public at an unfair disadvantage.

However, some researchers have suggested that we are still exposed to a kind of subliminal advertising every time we look at television (Radford, 1983). At the conscious level we take in a great deal about the characters, set, etc., but we may also take in information at the subconscious level and perceive details in the background which may influence our behaviour without our realizing it. For example, the decanter of whisky on a sideboard may, in susceptible individuals, trigger a desire for a drink without their even having noticed the decanter at the conscious level because it appeared on the screen in the background for such a short period of time.

Work on hypnosis has shed more light on this by demonstrating that under hypnosis people can remember many more details of an event than they can generally recall spontaneously. And a number of experiments have shown that by providing appropriate cues we can jog people's memory in such a way that they can remember details of events they were sure they had never noticed at the time; or we can encourage them to remember events which they believed they had forgotten long ago (Gregg, 1986). This work suggests that we all perceive a great deal more than we think we do (Coleman, 1987).

> **Look at the picture opposite for 20 seconds then cover it over and jot down all the details you can remember having seen. When you have listed all you can remember look back at the picture and see how accurate your perception of it was.**
>
> **Can you suggest any reasons why you remember certain things easily and other less easily or not at all?**
>
> **If you are working in a group compare the different things individuals in the group remembered.**

Selective Perception

When two individuals witness the same event they may give widely different accounts of it (Lofthus, 1979). This has made crime detection notoriously difficult – especially when evidence relies on individual descriptions of events or on identification of a suspect. It highlights another important aspect of perception – what we might call selective perception or selective attention.

We have already said that we remember things more easily if we have attended to them at the conscious level. We have also talked about the subliminal perception which occurs below the level of consciousness. What we haven't really looked at yet are the reasons why we attend to some things and not to others.

Part of the explanation lies in the attitudes we hold and, in the next chapter, we will look in some detail at how our attitudes affect perception. But there are a number of other reasons for selective perception which are less influenced by attitudes and more a feature of the perceptual stimulus itself. One of these is stimulus intensity.

Stimulus Intensity

Common sense tells us that if we hear a very loud noise or see a very bright light our attention will automatically be attracted to it. When a stimulus is very strong or intense, therefore, we are virtually forced to notice it and to perceive it consciously. The same applies when the stimulus is sudden. A sudden silence, for example, will attract our attention just as easily as a loud noise. A sudden loud noise is virtually guaranteed to make us sit up and take notice!

Variations in Stimulus

Even a loud noise can be ignored after a time if it is continuous, with little or no fluctuation in volume. After a time we become attuned to it and cease to notice it at the conscious level. This is just as well perhaps for those people who live near busy roads with the constant hum of traffic in the background!

> **Can you think of any strong continuous signals which you know are in your environment but which have become so familiar that you rarely notice them?**

When a stimulus is more variable – for example quiet periods alternating with periods of loud noise – it tends to be less easy to ignore. It might be possible to ignore a neon sign which was flashing at constant regular intervals, but it would be more difficult to ignore an intermittent flashing light. And most people have experienced the irritation of a tap dripping when they are trying to get off to sleep. In fact the noise of the tap dripping may not be loud but because it is irregular we not only notice it but almost find ourselves listening for the next drip whether we want to or not.

The ease with which intense or variable stimuli are perceived has a strong survival value since any sudden intense stimulus may signal possible danger. A change in stimuli makes us uncertain about what is happening and so alerts us to look more closely at what may be happening.

Physiological Factors

Another aspect of selective perception which has strong survival value is our instinctive need to respond to physiological changes in our bodies. When we are hungry, for example, we experience the effects of a drop in blood sugar level and the contractions which occur in the stomach. In order to satisfy our hunger we seek out food and, in the process, will be very attentive to any food-related stimuli which we may encounter. Hence the reason why people on a diet are told to eat before going shopping in order to prevent food items becoming particularly attractive to them! This is also the reason why people who are starving may report dreams of eating. Their perception is so firmly fixed on the need for food that they cannot attend to anything else even at the subconscious level of sleep.

To a lesser extent we can all be influenced to seek out food or drink by advertisements which – like the whisky decanter mentioned earlier – we perceive subliminally. This subliminal perception may cause us to attend to food-related stimuli even though we are not experiencing the physiological effects of hunger. The same applies to a whole range of stimuli which are related to other basic physiological needs such as avoidance of pain, the need for shelter, the need for comfort, the need for sleep, the sex urge or the need for stimulation. We will perceive and attend to those things which either answer a strong physiological need or remind us of the ways in which our needs may be met. This is why advertisers use sexy male or female bodies to attract attention to some of the most unlikely products!

> Compare the advertisements in magazines aimed at young women, the older married woman, and at men.
> What are the various stimuli used in the adverts to appeal to these different groups?
> How many of the adverts in the various publications make use of stimuli related to our physiological need for food, shelter, etc.

At the other extreme there is the phenomenon experienced by the person who is dying of thirst. Such a person may actually think he is seeing water when no water exists in reality. His perception is so firmly fixed on water that he can easily mistake some other image for the one he so desperately wants to see.

Again, to a lesser extent, we all tend to hear and see what we want to by the simple process of screening out those other signals which interfere with what we – consciously or subconsciously – want to attend to. If we are in a desperate hurry to catch a train, for example, we may not notice a pain in our leg which, were we in a more leisurely situation, might be felt quite acutely. Here we are making a choice (albeit a subconscious one) between seeking to satisfy our physical need – the need to attend to our pain – and a psychological need, our assumption about the importance of catching the train.

Can you recall any examples of occasions when you did not perceive a physical stimulus because you had other needs which you considered to be more important?

At what point did you again become aware of the need to attend to your physical well-being?

What were the changed circumstances which caused you to be more perceptive to the physical stimulus?

Situation Variable

Another thing which may cause a shift in perception is the situation in which the perceptual stimulus occurs. Think back to the example of mistaking your own reflection for someone else. You would have no expectancy set for seeing yourself in that situation and that, in itself, could reduce the likelihood of your recognizing yourself. In addition the situation of shopping would have created certain other expectations which would cause you to attend to those things relating to your reasons for being in the store in the first place. Had you been consciously looking in a mirror it would have been virtually impossible to avoid seeing and recognizing your own image.

Similarly when sitting in a room with other people you may not notice a whole range of fairly quiet sounds like the creak of a door or the ticking of a clock. When alone in the house on a dark night these sounds seem to assume more importance and to become much more noticeable, and possibly even frightening. The smell of burning will tend to be ignored if the individual knows that his neighbour is having a bonfire. When it occurs in the absence of a known source of fire the smell of burning will alert us very quickly to a possible danger.

Exactly the same sort of perceptual shift occurs when we believe ourselves or others to be in extreme danger. Quite a number of people have reported that when they were involved in or witnessed an accident which they were powerless to do anything about, their perception of time seemed to slow down. Events which, in reality, were occurring very quickly were perceived as taking place in slow motion. TV producers have cashed in on this phenomenon by filming sequences of high drama in slow motion, and the magazine advertisement for Scotchguard-treated carpets uses exactly the same device.

Familiarity

One further aspect of the stimulus which affects our perception is its level of familiarity. You may recall the example we gave of people who live near a busy road, and for whom the hum of traffic becomes so familiar that it ceases to be noticed. We also suggested that familiar household noises are not perceived unless the situation is one in which these small familiar noises are somehow heightened and invested with a new, and possibly threatening meaning.

A similar situation occurs in relation to everyday skills and activities. If, for example, we have become used to driving a car, we are perfectly capable of carrying out all the functions without really noticing what we are doing. It is as if these activities are carried out without our being conscious of them, leaving our conscious mind free to perceive the behaviour of other road-users, to listen to the radio or even use a car-phone. However, if we find ourselves in a tricky situation we may once more become conscious of our driving and our perception focuses in on coping with the difficult or unfamiliar situation (Nicholson & Lucas, 1984).

The same applies to our perception of people and places. We cease to notice the details of people and places with which we are familiar. After an absence from them we are often amazed at how much people have changed. Generally what we are seeing is not so much a sudden change in the people but simply a sharpening of our perception which allows us to see them in a less familiar and perhaps more accurate way.

Strangely enough, familiarity can also have the opposite effect of making us more alert to a perceptual stimulus. Experiments have shown that people are more likely to perceive a familiar stimulus when presented with a range of stimuli. They also tend to react more quickly. Subjects who believed themselves to be undertaking a test for speed of reaction were asked to press a buzzer as soon as they saw an image appearing on a screen. A list of nonsense words was then flashed up at varying intervals. In every case subjects pressed the buzzer more quickly when a nonsense word they had encountered in a previous exercise was presented. When real words were interspersed the speed of reaction was even faster for these (McClintock, 1976).

The reason for the apparent contradiction here seems to be that when familiar people or objects are seen in familiar and expected places or situations we become less alert to them and therefore perceive them less consciously. Put the familiar in an unfamiliar setting or look at it from a different viewpoint and our perception of it becomes sharper and more acute. Which is why all of us automatically turn our heads and listen if we hear our own names mentioned – especially if we are in a setting in which we are not expecting it.

And this brings us back to the example with which we started this chapter. We see our reflection so frequently, it becomes so familiar, that we do not see it objectively but perceive it with an overlay of all the attitudes we have about ourselves and our general appearance. When confronted unexpectedly with our reflection in an unfamiliar situation we are likely to see it differently, perhaps seeing ourselves 'as others see us' rather than as we believe ourselves to be.

In the next chapter we go on to look at some of these attitudes and values which arise out of what we believe about the world and our role in it, and we examine the ways in which attitudes and values affect communication with others.

Summary

1 Perception is information which is taken in by the senses, processed by the brain, stored in memory and produces some form of physical and mental activity.

2 Information obtained from the senses is limited by the way in which human sensory organs are constructed and by the absolute sense thresholds which determine the limits of our ability to take in sensory information.

3 There will be differences in how well or how badly an individual is capable of using each sense – either because of variations in the general functioning of each sense or because special training has developed a particular sense.

4 There will be differences between individuals in their sensory functioning – with some individuals being more handicapped in sensory functioning than others.

5 Physical sense organs determine what information we take in, but our brain interprets, categorizes and stores the information and enables us to make use of it in reacting to the world around us.

6 The way in which we react to any given perceptual stimulus will be determined not only by our sense and brain capacity, but also by the strength of the signal, the contrast or variation in it, its familiarity, the conditions under which it occurs and the extent to which it is competing for our attention with other stimuli which occur at the same time.

7 The other factors which determine how we perceive are either physiological – and determined by our particular physical state at any given time – or psychological. Psychological aspects include not only selectivity and expectancy sets but a whole range of attitudinal aspects which we will address in the next chapter.

REFERENCES

ARONSON, E. (1972): *The social animal*. Freeman

BARTLETT, F.C. (1932): *Remembering*. Cambridge University Press

COLEMAN, A.M. (1987): *Facts, fallacies and frauds in psychology*. Hutchinson

DIXON, N.F. (1971): *Subliminal perception: the nature of a controversy*. McGraw-Hill

GILLING, D. & BRIGHTWELL, R. (1982): *The human brain*. Orbis

GREGG, V.H. (1986): *Introduction to human memory*. Routledge & Kegan Paul

GREGORY, R.L. (1977): *Eye and brain*. Weidenfeld & Nicolson

KELLY, H.H. (1950): The warm-cold variable in first impressions of persons. *Journal of Personality* 18, 431–9

KRAMER, L. (eds) (1974): *Advances in the study of communication and affect*. Vol. 1. Plenum Press

LOFTHUS, E.F. (1979): *Eyewitness testimony*. Harvard University Press

McCLINTOCK, A.B. (1976): Response thresholds. Unpublished Dip. Ed. Research, University of Glasgow

MITCHELL, T.R. & LARSON, J.R. (1987): *People in organisations*. McGraw-Hill

NAYLOR, J., PRITCHARD, R. & ILGING, G. (1980): *A theory of behaviour in organisations*. Academic Press

NICHOLSON, J. & LUCAS, M. (1984): *All in the mind*. Methuen

PIAGET, J. & INHELDER, B. (1958): *The growth of logical thinking*. Routledge & Kegan Paul

RADFORD, G.P. (1983): *Subliminal persuasion*. Occasional Paper. Communication Studies Dept., Sheffield City Polytechnic

ZALKIND, S.S. & COSTELLO, T.V. (1962): Perception: implications for administration. *Administrative Science Quarterly* 7, 218–35

CHAPTER TWO
ATTITUDES AND VALUES

In the previous chapter we looked at some of the things which govern how we perceive ourselves and the world around us. This chapter deals with two other aspects of psychology which are fundamental to the process of communication – the values we hold and the attitudes we adopt to express these values in our verbal and non-verbal behaviour. No matter how much or how little we say, our tone of voice, our posture, the words we choose, and even the words we avoid, all say something about our attitudes and values. This applies whether we are in direct face-to-face conversation, communicating via the written word, or using pictures or signs to convey our meaning. The hearer or reader also has a set of attitudes and values and will tend to interpret our attitudes on the basis of his or her own. This can create confusion or misunderstanding and may even lead to a total breakdown in communication.

Read over the previous paragraph again and try to decide what attitudes the writers are expressing in it.

What assumptions are they making about you, the reader?

How do you feel about the tone they have adopted?

On the basis of reading this book so far, have you arrived at any conclusions concerning the age, or the appearance, or the character of the authors?

If you are working in a group, perhaps you could compare your answers with those of others.

As authors we have no way of knowing how you answered the questions, but we can say a little about what we intended. For example, the fact that we mentioned the possibility of communication breakdown suggests that we feel this is a bad thing. For us, the idea of good communication has a certain positive value; whereas confusion, misunderstanding and communication breakdown are to be avoided. As we have made an assumption that the reader is positively motivated not only to read the text but to re-read and discuss it in the context of the questions asked, we obviously think that doing so has something of value to offer. We value the involvement of the reader, even though we have no idea who or where the reader is. By suggesting the task we demonstrate our attitude towards the reader.

But what about the questions on age or appearance or character? Surely you cannot answer these with any degree of certainty? Of course not! All you can do is make a number of inferences based on your own general attitudes about people who write books of this kind. Because you do not know the authors personally you have to resort to a *stereotyped* picture of what authors are like, how they think and how they behave. And this stereotype will be based on attitudes and values which you have developed over a number of years.

We will return to the concept of stereotypes later in the chapter, but, first, let us look a little more closely at what we mean by attitudes and values and how we aquire them.

The Development of Value Systems

Over the past 30 or 40 years there has been considerable controversy among psychologists as to whether human beings develop in the way that they do as a result of genetic endowment, or maturation or as a result of being influenced by the environment into which they are born. This controversy has not yet been resolved, but at the present time the evidence from research suggests that how we develop as individual human beings cannot be explained by a single theory but by a complex interaction of the various theories. The majority of psychologists today would seem to believe that human development is partly controlled by the genes we have inherited from our parents, partly by our instinctive need to obtain food, shelter, stimulation, etc., and partly by what we experience in life (Burns, 1982).

For example, some children are born with a thyroid deficiency which is passed on genetically from parents to children. In the past doctors didn't realize this and children were left untreated, with the result that they gradually became more and more mentally handicapped and unable to lead any kind of normal life (Thomas, 1978). Now doctors can recognize the condition and treat it effectively so that children can develop normally. We could say, therefore, that the presence or absence of mental handicap in these children results from a combination of inherited genes which *cause* thyroid deficiency and experiences after birth which *determine* how the deficiency will affect the child's development.

The same kind of process occurs in relation to a whole range of other inherited characteristics such as good hearing and perfect eyes, our capacity to feel and respond to pain, whether we are active or passive, and so on. Because of the individual differences in sensory acuity which we discussed in the previous chapter we will all react differently to the world around us and we will have different experiences of the world. What we experience after birth may determine how far these inherited characteristics will be expressed later in our attitudes and value systems.

Those experiences which seem to answer a need in us we regard as pleasurable and want to repeat. We want to avoid those experiences which are unpleasant or painful. And, because human beings are herd animals with a natural capacity for imitation, we will copy the behaviour of the people around us. In order to identify with the people we like or admire, we may adopt some of their values and reject the values of those who are different.

At first our value systems are fairly crude. Those objects, events or people which bring us pleasure come to have a positive value for us. We think of them as good. Those which bring pain, or are unrewarding, have a negative value and are regarded as bad. Gradually, we begin to make a distinction between more or less good, more or less bad; or good in some circumstances but not good in others. Eventually we develop a value system which is complex, and often contradictory.

We may, for example, value friendship and behave in such a way as to ensure that we have friends and remain loyal to them. We may also value honesty and try to ensure that we are as honest as possible at all times. Generally these two values may not cause conflicts. But what happens when a friend asks for our opinion and we have to make a choice between telling the truth and risking hurting the feelings of our friend, perhaps even damaging the friendship?

> **Can you think of any situations in your own life when you had to make a choice between two conflicting values?**
> **How did making that choice affect how you felt, what you said and how you behaved?**
> **Would you decide to behave the same or differently if faced with a similar choice now?**
> **What does your answer tell you about your value system?**

Attitudes

What we do, say, think and feel in any specific instance will be determined by how we balance out the various aspects of our value systems. Even when choices are made at the subconscious, rather than the conscious level, they still manifest themselves in thoughts, feelings or behaviour.

> *It is this combination of thought, feelings and potential for action, based on how we balance out the various aspects of our value systems, which we describe as attitudes.*

Other people cannot know for certain what we are thinking or feeling, but they can observe what we do and say, and will make judgements about us on this basis. When we say that someone is acting out of character what we are observing is behaviour which doesn't fit in with the pattern of behaviour we have come to expect from that person, and we may therefore have to revise our opinion of their attitudes and values. If we feel unable to judge what someone might say or do in a particular situation it might be that we do not know the person well enough to have formed an opinion of their attitudes; or it might be that the person has such an inconsistent pattern of attitudes that we find it difficult to make any assumptions about their behaviour.

> **Try this task. Write down a number of different qualities which an individual might value – for example love, or ambition, or intelligence, or cleanliness, etc. Pick a pair of these at random and try to think of situations in which the individual might experience a conflict between these values. Suggest a number of different ways in which a person might behave in trying to resolve this conflict. How would the language used differ in the various situations? Which of the behaviours would be compatible with each other and could fit together to show a consistent attitude pattern?**

Labelling and Classifying

In the exercise above we asked you to suggest which speech and behaviour patterns you would regard as being compatible with each other. In order to do this you had to draw on your previous experience of the type of behaviours normally found together in one individual, and the type of person you would expect to exhibit these behaviours. In other words, you were basing your assumptions on the kind of expectancy sets which we discussed in Chapter One.

In that chapter we also noted that these expectancy sets are made possible by the brain's capacity to store, label and classify information. This ability is one which all human beings possess. Without it we would have great difficulty in developing intellectually since we would have no way of using previous experience to help us make sense of new experience. We would be unable to use a hierarchical language and concept system, and would have to rely instead on labelling everything individually without cross-reference.

To illustrate what we mean by a hierarchical language system, try this task.

> **An apple may be classified as a fruit. Fruit can be classified as food. Food can be classified as body fuel. Each gives a more generalized category into which the word apple might fit. Similarly, it is possible to give more and more precise classifications – not just apple, but red apple, juicy red apple, big juicy red apple, etc. See how many categories you can find for the words dog, house, love and fear. Could you find an even more complex category that might include all of these words? Could you draw a diagram which shows the most general category at the top and gradually subdivides to show how each category relates to the others?**

The process of labelling and classifying starts in childhood, and becomes more complex and refined as we develop. Young children may have categories which are too narrow – refusing, for example, to label as dog any dog which is different from the dog they are used to. They may also have over-extended categories – for example calling every four-legged animal dog regardless of what it is. Gradually the labels become more specific and the categories more defined so that as adults we can carry out with ease the kind of complex classification task suggested above.

The Development of Personal Constructs

Labelling and classification enable us to build up a mental picture of all the events, people and objects with which we come into contact. We could call these mental pictures *personal constructs* – literally the way we have constructed our own personal mental world out of all that we have experienced and perceived (Green, 1975).

To get some idea of your own personal constructs try this task:

Read over the list which follows, and as you read each word write down the words which seems to sum up your emotional reactions, and your mental picture for each word:

Dog
Pig
Teddy bear
House
Home
Danger.

Try the same thing with words of your own choosing and you should soon find that almost every word conjures up some picture and some emotional reaction that will reveal your attitude to that word, and to the general type of which the word is an example.

Stereotyping

In everyday life we often apply the first or most obvious label to a person or event rather than trying to give a precise and accurate description. For example, when we meet someone for the first time we obtain only a superficial impression, but in order to make sense of the experience we may label the person according to his dress, race, accent or some other obvious feature. If we then go on to get to know the person as an individual we will devise a much more complex classification of the type of person he is.

If we don't get to know the person there is a good chance that he will become fixed in our mind as an example of a more general type – a teenager, a bank manager, a foreigner, etc. We may then assume that he will display *all* the characteristics we expect to find in that type of person.

What we believe these characteristics to be will depend on the attitudes and values we have developed in relation to that type. Our emotional reaction to the person will also be based on the way we have learned to relate to people of that type rather than responding to the person as an individual.

> *A stereotype is the term we use to describe the mental picture, the emotional reactions and the behaviour we display when we classify according to general type, rather than attending to the specific characteristics displayed by an individual example of that type.*

Stereotyping provides a convenient and very necessary technique for making quick judgements and giving speedy reactions. But, just as the young child's classification may be too narrow or too broad, so adult stereotypes may be equally limited, causing us sometimes to arrive at conclusions which are not only wrong but may be very damaging to interpersonal communication.

What stereotyped characteristics do you associate with the following people:

Shop stewards
Politicians
Bank managers
Musicians?

If you tried this exercise in company with others, you would probably find that there were a number of similarities – as well as individual differences – in the characteristics chosen. The differences are easy to account for since each individual has had different experiences and has therefore acquired a unique personal construct relating to that stereotype. What is less easy to explain is why there are so many common stereotypes which people recognize, even if they don't always agree with them.

The Development of Common Stereotypes

One explanation is that, as stereotypes are based on obvious superficial features, they contain a grain of truth. The trouble is that this grain of truth is often overlaid with a whole range of assumptions which may result in a mental picture which is very far from being the truth.

For example, a man in a kilt is automatically recognized as a Scotsman even though nowadays few Scots wear kilts. Whisky is one of Scotland's major exports and many Scots do drink whisky. Put the two features together and you get the typical stereotype of the drunken Scotsman!

> Go back to the previous list and see if you can work out the obvious features which have given rise to the stereotypes associated with the people in the list.
>
> What are the assumptions which have been made in each case?
>
> Why do you think these assumptions have been made?

The Influence of a Common Culture

One reason for the existence of commonly held stereotypes and assumptions is the fact that human beings are herd animals, living in groups and dependent on other members of the group for their survival. Just as we develop some of our values as a result of identifying with and copying others in our society, so we learn to judge others by how far they seem to fit in with or diverge from the normal behaviour seen in groups in our country, district or social group. Those who seem to fit in with the group norms are regarded favourably. Those outside the group may be regarded less favourably.

Negative Stereotypes

Anyone who is obviously different may be treated with suspicion. It is tempting to assume that they will somehow have a different set of values from ours, and will display behaviour which threatens the security of our group. There is, therefore, a natural tendency to avoid them rather than to seek to get to know them as individuals. And, of course, it is easier to avoid someone if we can find reasons to support our behaviour. Thus if someone is taller, or smaller or more slant-eyed or displays some other obvious feature that is out of keeping with the group norms, we may decide he is not to be trusted, or is overbearing, or arrogant or any one of a range of negative qualities. Over a period of time the group begins to believe that this particular feature of appearance really does signify the negative quality they have ascribed to it. Myths of this sort are passed down from parents to children and between members of a group until eventually they are accepted as fact by the majority of people who share a common culture and the original reason for the myth is forgotten.

> Can you think of any reasons to account for the fact that Scots are often regarded as mean? Or the Irish as stupid? Or the French as unclean?

Can you identify any myths of this kind which you grew up with – even if you have since rejected them – and can you find any reasons to account for the existence of these myths or stereotypes in your culture?

If you have rejected some of the common myths and stereotypes can you explain why?

One reason for rejecting the common myths and stereotypes is personal experience. As we said right at the start of this chapter, you will probably be very wary of making assumptions about authors as a type if you have met several and know that they are very different. Nevertheless, you may still be able to recognize the stereotypes of authors when you are exposed to these stereotypes in the media.

The Influence of the Media

In the modern world we are surrounded by the mass media of communication – books, newspapers, television and so on. To establish a character quickly in the mind of their audience media productions often rely on the use of an obvious or superficial characteristic. When the stereotypes presented in the media fit with the stereotypes we are familiar with this may help to reinforce our belief that these stereotypes are true. The presentation of stereotypes in the media may also represent a way by which stereotypes can be developed among those who, until seeing the media presentation, had no fixed view of a particular type and no personal experience of people within the type.

Look at one episode of a popular series on TV. Do the characters seem to be complex 'real-life' people, or are they popular stereotypes of how people of a particular race, class, creed or culture behave? To what extent do any of the stereotypes portrayed fit with your own experience of meeting people from that particular background?

If the stereotypes shown on the media do not seem to reflect what our own experience has led us to believe we are likely to recognize that what we are being shown are simply stereotypes and not real portrayals of real individuals. And the fact that we do have access to a wide range of media allows us to gain more experience of other cultures, races and social groups. As we learn more about others from documentaries and books we begin to reject the simple stereotypes, even though we may still recognize that these stereotypes exist.

Can you identify any stereotypes which you have recently seen portrayed in advertisements?

Can you identify any media portrayed stereotypes which have changed in recent years?

Can you identify any information which you have obtained from the mass media which has changed your attitudes towards an individual or group, or caused you to reject common stereotypes?

The Halo Effect

So far we have concentrated mainly on negative stereotypes, but, of course, positive stereotypes are equally possible. If someone shows obvious features of dress, speech or general appearance which suggest that they will be 'our type' we will tend to find that person acceptable and to assume that they will display all the qualities that we personally like or admire. In a number of studies, for example, it has been shown that when people were asked to rate others on their level of attractiveness, one of two things happened. They either rated the individual according to the current fashion of attractiveness as shown in film stars and others featured on the media; or they rated as attractive people who seemed to be like themselves in some ways. When asked to rate the 'attractive' people on a whole range of other qualities, those who were seen as more attractive were perceived to possess more of other desirable qualities like intelligence, a sense of humour, or kindliness (Bem, 1970). This is known as the 'halo effect' – one known good quality causing us to see a halo or ring of other good qualities around it, which may be as much an illusion as the ring of light haloing the moon.

Can you think of any common situations in which taking a decision based on either positive or negative stereotypes could lead to unfairness and discrimination?

When Stereotypes Become Prejudices

Deeply entrenched stereotypes can be described as prejudices. Prejudice is a particularly dangerous form of stereotyping because it is so resistant to change. There is also some evidence to show that although prejudices may be acquired in much the same way as stereotypes, they are accompanied by a stronger emotional reaction. For example, a man who is afraid that his own role in society may be threatened if women gain more power may display considerable prejudice against working wives or women in managerial positions (Fitzpatrick, 1987).

Another research study has shown that feelings of anger or aggression or frustration may be relieved if they are directed against those towards whom we have strong negative stereotypes, or against those whom we believe to be less powerful and therefore unable to retaliate against us (Weatherley, 1961). The stereotyped group becomes the scapegoat we blame for what is happening in our lives to make us feel bad. This is particularly the case if we don't know why we feel angry or frustrated, or if we feel powerless to express our emotions and confront the person or situation that we know to be the cause.

For example, football fans who become frustrated by the performance of their team on the field may resort to hurling abuse at the referee or the supporters of the other side. The person who feels angry at the boss may relieve his anger by blaming it all on the government, or the class system or some other stereotype which can provide a convenient scapegoat.

A study by Christopher Bagley for the Race Relations Board also showed that fear and anger can create conditions favourable to prejudice and scapegoating (Bagley, 1970). In this case the fear was that immigrants to Great Britain would 'steal' the jobs and homes that could have gone to white British, and that the way of life and values of the immigrant communities would destroy traditional British values and customs. Immigrants became the scapegoat for more general anger and frustration with lack of employment and poor environmental conditions. In areas with a large immigrant population prejudice among white people seemed to be stronger than in areas where there were relatively few immigrants.

At first glance this seems to contradict the view that as we get to know people better we reject the common stereotypes in favour of a more complex and individualized mental picture. If white people have a large number of black neighbours then it seems logical to assume that they would get to know at least some of them as people and that this would reduce negative stereotypes. However, what seems to happen is the opposite. As long as the 'different' members remain in a minority people will either avoid them as we suggested above, or will get to know them as people. When numbers in the minority group increase they are perceived as more of a threat by members of the established group. The resultant feelings of fear and insecurity among the established group seem to serve to turn negative stereotypes or avoidance into prejudice and actively hostile attitudes.

Another of Bagley's findings was that people who had gone through a process of further or higher education were generally less racially prejudiced, and that the younger people in this educated group tended to show least prejudice – perhaps because the process of education helps people to recognize and question their attitudes and prejudices, and partly because young people at this stage in their lives are still developing their value systems and attitudes.

Can you identify any educational influence in your own life which has caused you to question your attitudes, stereotypes and prejudices?

What form did this influence take?
Can you work out the stages you went through in the process of attitude change?

The Theory of Cognitive Dissonance

One theory which has been advanced to explain the process of attitude change is that of cognitive dissonance. Put at its simplest this theory suggests that when we behave in a way which is consistent with our values and beliefs we experience a feeling of mental well-being. When we behave in a way which is inconsistent with our values and beliefs we experience a mental state of confusion and dissatisfaction. Festinger (1957) called this unpleasant mental state cognitive dissonance. He predicted that whenever we experience dissonance we seek to reduce it – by changing our beliefs and attitudes, by changing our behaviour, or by changing both to bring them more into line with each other.

We gave an example of dissonance earlier in this chapter when we mentioned the conflict of values that may occur when one feels forced to choose between attitudes of friendship and honesty. In this situation the very act of making a choice may help to reduce the dissonance. By choosing one course of action we are mentally revising our value system and determining to which of the two to give priority.

Dissonance also occurs when we are confronted with a situation in which someone does not behave in a way which accords with our stereotypes or prejudice. We may reduce dissonance by the simple expedient of assuming that this person is unrepresentative. If, on the other hand, we find ourselves having to co-operate with the person as a colleague at work it may be difficult to maintain prejudice and easier to reduce dissonance by changing our prejudiced attitude. This is particularly likely to occur if co-operation takes place in a common cause which both regard as important, or in a situation of shared adversity.

For example, an American study showed that the presence of black students in a white university was not sufficient to reduce prejudice against black people. It was only when the students began to work with each other in a project which involved helping local disabled people that prejudice began to be reduced and both black and white students started to see each other as people rather than stereotypes (Gahagan, 1975).

Can you think of any other examples of cognitive disso-
nance involving a conflict between behaviour and values?
Can you identify any examples in your own life of situa-
tions in which cognitive dissonance caused you to modify
your behaviour, your attitudes or both?

If you are in a group or paired situation could you role-play any situations which exemplify the cognitive dissonance which occurs when a group or individual behaves in a way which is out of keeping with the prejudice or stereotyped attitudes others may have against them?

Prejudice also helps to explain why people perceive the same event in different ways. In a study by Allport & Postman (1954) subjects were invited to describe a picture in which a white man was holding an open razor in his hand and arguing with a black man. As the story was passed from individual to individual details of the story changed. Those prejudiced against black people remembered the razor in the hand of the black man and it was he who was seen to be threatening the white man.

Selective Exposure

In the previous chapter we discussed the selectivity of our perception. One of the reasons for this selectivity lies in the fact that we allow ourselves to be exposed to only those aspects of life which confirm our view of the world. People who are already committed to an idea will be the most likely to pay attention when such ideas are broadcast and advertised.

Those who are already interested and committed to a healthy life are the ones who will be most likely to notice and act upon the information (Stirckland, 1982). Political campaigns designated to create public awareness are most often watched by those who are already responsive to the political party (Berger & Chaffee, 1987). While those who have recently purchased new consumer goods are likely to notice and read an advert for the particular commodity they have just purchased (Wheldall, 1975).

Quickly turn over the pages of a magazine.

Jot down all the adverts you can remember having seen as you flicked through it.

Do any of the ads you noted confirm any of things we have been saying about perception and attitudes?

If not, can you explain why you remembered the ones you did – and have you checked to make sure they really are there?

If you are working in a group it would be interesting to see what the differences were in the ads noticed, and why.

Selective Avoidance

The opposite of selective exposure is selective avoidance. On the whole, people do not voluntarily place themselves in situations where they feel ill at ease. They tend to avoid people they dislike, or feel they have little in common with, and they tend to avoid hearing or seeing information which is at odds with their own attitudes. People who smoke will tend to avoid reading research reports about its damaging effects and may even try to seek out information which highlights the benefits of smoking. And teachers have noted that it is frequently the parents of children who are likely to have a good school report who turn up on parents' nights. The parents whose children are doing less well may avoid turning up to have the bad news confirmed!

Discounting

Another way in which we can avoid information we don't want to accept is to try to suggest that the person who put out the information is not a credible source. People who want to go on drinking and driving, for example, may suggest that the statistics quoted in the paper are biased and unreliable – 'nobody believes anything that is printed in that rag!'

A further way is to try to minimize the importance or accuracy of the information itself, or to say something like 'it might be true for X but it isn't true for me'. When the government was trying to influence motorists to wear seat belts surveys were carried out to find why, despite millions of pounds of advertising money being spent, only 40 per cent of drivers wore seat belts. The typical kind of discounting was 'well I knew a friend who was trapped in his car by a seat belt so I wouldn't wear one' or 'I've been driving for years without one and I've never had so much as a scratch, why should I need one now?'

> Can you think of any situations in which you have engaged in any of the behaviours described above in order to avoid or discount information which made you feel uncomfortable about something you were doing?
>
> What kind of thing did you say to yourself in order to justify what you were doing?
>
> Have you ever ignored what your rational mind knew to be the case because your felt strongly about something?
>
> How did this affect what you said and did?

Conformity

Another type of human behaviour, which is closely linked to prejudice, is conformity. *Conformity may be described as a willingness to adopt the same behaviours and attitudes as those seen in other people.*

In order to experience a sense of 'belonging' to a particular group an individual may willingly adopt the group's values and behaviour. Sometimes, however, an individual will conform to the behaviour of those around him even when they are comparative strangers. It seems that many human beings don't like to stand out in a crowd or seem to be different from those around, and they have a strong urge to conform to the behaviour of other people simply to avoid making themselves conspicuous. (Ornstein, 1986). People will also avoid becoming involved in a situation if they can shrug off their responsibility by assuming that someone else will do something. When an apparent murder took place outside a block of flats in New York, residents must have heard or seen something, yet there was no call to the police and no one came out to help or investigate (Coleman, 1987).

Another study showed that some people will change their opinion in order to conform to the majority view (Asch, 1951). In Asch's experiment a group of people were shown a picture of a series of lines and asked to choose those which were most alike in length. All but one of the people in the group had been primed previously to give a wrong answer. The one who had not been primed did not know this and at first gave the correct answer. But, when he heard the others, he changed his mind and agreed to accept that the others were right.

We tried some similar experiments with our own students and found that most of our students conformed in the same way as Asch describes. There were, however, one or two students who refused to conform. In every case there were students who had very strong leadership qualities. What our experiments seem to show is that although most people will conform to the majority view, natural leaders may prefer to persuade others to adopt their viewpoint rather than conforming to the views of the majority.

Try this experiment. And don't cheat! Only turn to p.34 for the answer when you have completed the task.

Without measuring them, which of the two lines shown below would you estimate to be the longer?

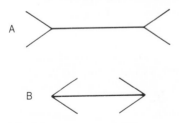

Fig 2.1

Those who saw this illusion in the chapter on perception may be pretty sure they know the right answer. Even if you think you do, please turn to p.34 anyway.

What we have said about conformity so far seems to suggest that it may be wrong to conform. Clearly there are occasions when this is so, especially when conformity involves adopting prejudices or behaviour which can harm other people. But, of course, there are many many occasions when conformity is not only right but necessary. If we all decided that we were not going to conform to the highway code there would be chaos on the roads! And a democratic society can exist only if everyone agrees to abide by and conform to majority rule.

Compliance

There are times, however, when we show conformity in what we say and do without really being willing to identify with or accept the attitudes we are expressing in our speech and behaviour. We may, for example, be afraid to go against the majority. Or we may be prepared to go along with the majority in order to gain some kind of reward.

> *Conformity which occurs as a result of fear of punishment or in anticipation of a reward without being accompanied by a willing acceptance of the values and attitudes underlying that behaviour would be described as compliance.*

At the simplest level compliance may occur when we have to obey the rules of someone in authority over us even if we do not agree with the rules. Compliance can also occur if we feel that the other person is a credible authority. We may not necessarily agree with the authority but we may feel that we do not have the knowledge, or even the right, to challenge that authority and so we comply with what is expected of us.

A number of experimental studies have demonstrated this quite dramatically. For example, one researcher asked volunteers to give electric shocks to another person who was described as having a weak heart. The volunteers were told that the shocks were a necessary part of a memory and learning test and that they could do no real harm. The volunteers could not know that the person who seemed to be receiving the shocks was, in fact, simply acting. What was interesting was that virtually all of the volunteers continued to administer more and more powerful shocks when asked to do so by the researcher in spite of the fact that the person in the chair seemed to be in pain (Milgram, 1974).

More recent studies have shown that people not only show conformity in laboratory situations where they feel they have to obey the rules of the experiment. They also do so in real-life settings. For example, nurses complied with instructions given by doctors even though the instructions seemed highly suspect and out of keeping with normal hospital practice (Ornstein, 1986). Perhaps this also helps to explain some of the reasons why atrocities are committed in times of war by those who are 'only obeying orders' (Arendt, 1963).

> **Can you think of any occasions in your own life when you have complied with what was expected of you even though you did not agree with or believe in what you were doing?**
>
> **What did you say to yourself to explain or rationalize your behaviour?**

Attitude Change

It is relatively easy to explain or justify compliant behaviour when the rewards or threats are great, but a good number of research studies have shown that people will often comply even when the threats or rewards are small. What seems to happen in this situation is that people find it difficult to justify compliance and therefore change their attitudes in order to reduce dissonance and demonstrate to themselves that they really believed in what they were doing!

For example, students who were asked to undertake a very boring experiment for quite good pay reported that the experiment was boring. Those who were given very small payments, however, reported the experiment as being quite interesting. It was as if those who couldn't justify why they were taking part in the experiment on the grounds of monetary rewards had to find some other means of justifying their behaviour – hence their perception of the task as less boring (Fishbein & Ajzen, 1967).

Similar changes in attitude seem to occur when individuals are asked to express a viewpoint with which they don't really agree. If they can find a good reason for doing so – for example a strong desire to win a debate – they can express with conviction views that they don't really hold. If there are no really strong reasons or rewards they may well come to believe in what they are saying. Perhaps this explains the conviction with which politicians can present party policies which they may have disagreed with earlier in their careers!

Attitudes as Part of Total Communication

We will return to this, and many other aspects of attitude change, in later chapters when we look at non-verbal communication and the communication processes which occur in groups and organizations. In this chapter we have tried to show that attitudes have an important part to play in virtually every aspect of human communication. Whether we are aware of them or not, our attitudes colour the way we perceive other people, the assumptions we make about their personalities, and the reasons we attribute to their behaviour. This in turn affects not only our choice of those with whom we wish to communicate but also what we say and how we say it. It affects how we talk about other people, and how we react to portrayals of others in the media. It affects the extent to which we are prepared to believe what people say or to act on their instructions. And our beliefs about other people's attitudes to us affect how we relate to them in a whole variety of interpersonal communication situations.

Summary

1 In our formative years we develop a system of beliefs and values which determines our attitudes towards everything and everyone in our environment. These attitudes do not remain fixed but change throughout our lives as we encounter new people, ideas and experiences.

2 The interrelationship between perception and attitudes is a complex one – our ability to interpret sensory information being dependent not only on the acuity of our sense organs but also on the way we distort sensory information to bring it into line with our attitudes.

3 When we behave in a way which is inconsistent with our attitudes, or if we receive new information which seems to conflict with what we want to hear or what we already believe, we feel uneasy and seek to reduce this unease by changing our behaviour or beliefs, or by other strategies such as avoiding conflicting information, or discrediting the source of the information.

4 Attitudes which are based on obvious or superficial features which we attribute to a particular type of person are called stereo-types. These stereotypes may be either positive or negative and may be upheld by or reflected in the media.

5 Stereotypes which are resistant to change and are accompanied by a strong emotional reaction are regarded as prejudices.

6 Even those who do not feel prejudiced may display prejudiced behaviour in order to conform with the majority or with groups and individuals with whom they wish to be identified.

7 Conformity is not restricted to prejudiced behaviour. In any democratic society it is necessary to conform to the rules and norms of that society, and most people will conform because they hold attitudes roughly in line with expected behaviour.

8 Compliance is outward conformity – individuals conform because of fear, promise of reward or some other strong incentive, rather than because they accept the attitudes being demonstrated in their behaviour.

9 When individuals comply with expected behaviour without having a good reason for doing so, they may either invent a reason or change their attitudes to justify their compliant behaviour.

10 The attitudes we hold pervade all our communication behaviours and are an important part of the total process of perception and communication.

REFERENCES

ALLPORT, G.W. & POSTMAN, F.H. (1954): *The nature of prejudice*. Addison-Wesley

ARENDT, H. (1963) *Eichmann in Jerusalem: a report on the banality of evil*. Viking Press

ASCH, S.J. (1951): Effects of group pressure on the modification and distortion of judgements. In Guetzkow, H. (ed.), *Groups, leadership and men*. Carnegie Press

BAGLEY, C. (1970): *Prejudice in five English boroughs*. Institute of Race Relations

BEM, D.J. (1970): *Beliefs, attitudes, and human affairs*. Brooks-Cole

BERGER, C.R. & CHAFFEE, S.H. (eds) (1987): *Handbook of communication science*. Sage

BERSCHEID, E. (1985): Interpersonal attraction. In Lindzey, D. & Aronson, E. (eds), *Handbook of social psychology*, 3rd edn, Vol. 2, 157–215. Academic Press

BURNS, R.B. (1982): *Essential psychology*. MTP Press

COLEMAN, A.M. (1987): *Facts, fallacies and frauds in psychology*. Hutchinson

FESTINGER, L. (1957): *A theory of cognitive dissonance*. Row Peterson

FISHBEIN, M. & AJZEN, I. (1967): *Belief, attitude, intention and behaviour*. Addison-Wesley

FITZPATRICK, M.A. (1987): Marital Interaction. In Berger & Chaffee 1987, 564–681

GAGAHAN, J. (1975): *Interpersonal and group behaviour*. Methuen

GREEN, J. (1975): *Thinking and language*. Methuen

MILGRAM, S. (1974): *Obedience to authority*. Tavistock

ORNSTEIN, R. (1986): *Multimind*. Macmillan

STRICKLAND, D. (1982): Alcohol advertising; orientations and influence. *Journal of advertising, quarterly review of marketing communication* 1, 307–19

THOMAS, D. (1978): *The social psychology of childhood disability*. Methuen

WEATHERLEY, D. (1961): Anti-Semitism and the expression of fantasy aggression. *Journal of Abnormal and Social Psychology* 62, 454–7

WHELDALL, K. (1975): *Social behaviour*. Methuen

Answer to Question on p.29

Line A is longer than line B. When a group of students familiar with this illusion was shown the figure they automatically assumed that the two were the same length. When shown several versions and asked if they were sure that they were the same length, they became uncertain and the majority conformed to the views expressed by a few students who were convinced that they had the right answers. When they finally measured the lines they found that the 'convinced' students were not, on the whole, right. Perhaps you might like to make up a few test examples of the illusion and try this experiment in perception and conformity for yourself.

CHAPTER THREE
VERBAL AND NON-VERBAL COMMUNICATION

In Chapters One and Two we looked at some of the ways in which perception of people's speech and behaviour can be influenced by attitudes, stereotypes or prejudices. We hear a particular set of words, but how we interpret and understand them will depend on more than the words. The tone of voice, the accent, accompanying gestures or facial expressions will all influence our understanding. Superficial features such as dress, colour of skin and other physical characteristics will also affect how we understand and respond.

The actual words used would be regarded as *verbal communication*. All the other features would come into the category of *non-verbal communication* – or NVC for short.

> **Working with a partner, sit facing each other and for the next 60 seconds you may look at each other but avoid saying anything or deliberately communicating with each other in any way.**

Most people would probably feel that those involved in this exercise had not been communicating with each other – had, in fact, simply been sitting in silence. Admittedly there was no *intention* to communicate. Just the opposite! But, in spite of this, some communication almost certainly did take place.

> **Can each of you work out what was communicated by the other, and by what means?**
> **Don't compare notes at this stage, simply jot down what you noted.**

Each of you may have noted a number of things – for example, the 'messages' sent by your partner's clothing, and small changes in facial expression that confirmed that your partner was trying to avoid communicating or laughing. From the positions you adopted in your seats you may have deduced that your partner was tense or relaxed, nervous or bored. So, even in a situation in which people are trying *not* to communicate, a great deal of information may still be passing between them.

The trouble with information which has been obtained in this way is that it is difficult to be sure that the deductions you have made are accurate. To what extent were the 'messages' you took out of the situation an accurate reflection of what your partner was actually thinking or feeling; and to what extent were you simply interpreting the 'messages' in line with your own attitudes?

> **Take a few minutes to discuss with your partner how accurate the 'messages' that passed between you actually were.**

We will come back and look at the question of accuracy later in the chapter. But first let us consider in more detail the relationship between intention to communicate and the process of communication itself.

Intention

You may have noticed that we've put the word 'messages' in inverted commas in the text above. This is because we normally think of a message as part of a deliberate communication process; whereas what we have been considering is a process of communication which seems to be taking place without deliberate intent – almost as if messages were being received without the sender having been aware of sending them.

Another way of looking at it would be to think of this type of communication as a process in which both partners search for meaning and try to interpret it in a non-verbal situation, rather than as a linear process in which messages are deliberately sent and received.

Verbal communication almost always has a deliberate intention – that of sending some message, to someone, somewhere, regardless of whether the message is ever received or understood by those for whom it is intended. Non-verbal communication can also be deliberate; for example, when we nod in agreement, smile in greeting, point to a sign, and so on. We may also dress in a particular way with the intention of conveying information to others – as, for example, when our clothes show that we belong to a club or organization, or that we can afford to buy designer-label rather than mass-produced, or want to draw attention to a particular aspect of our physical appearance! Sometimes, too, we are forced to wear clothing which conveys a message as part of our contract of employment – police or armed-forces uniforms being obvious examples.

There are many occasions, however, when we are not aware of an intention to convey a message by non-verbal means. We are not trying to communicate with anyone in particular, and not conscious of the fact that others may be interpreting our non-verbal signals and investing them with meaning. For example, this is true when our clothes are not chosen to project a particular impression but are simply the result of having grabbed the first thing in our wardrobe that was clean! Similarly we may not be aware, when talking to someone we agree with, that our posture is mirroring that of the other person; or that the emotions we are experiencing are being conveyed by changes in facial expressions.

Working with a different partner from before, if possible, discuss between you which aspects of your appearance today represent a deliberate attempt to convey a particular message about yourself, and which do not.

Leakage

There are also times when we are deliberately intending to send a particular message, but the information we give out at the conscious level may be modified or contradicted by other non-verbal signals which we are not aware of sending. This extra information, as it were, leaks out. An example of this might be the situation in which an individual was trying very hard to give the impression of being relaxed and confident, but leaked the fact that he was nervous by the tension in his facial expressions. Another example might be that of the person who wanted to convey the impression of warmth in greeting another by smiling, but the warmth of the smile was not reflected in the eyes which remained cold or unresponsive.

High-speed photography has enabled us to observed the minute and very rapid micro-facial changes in expression that occur when people are engaged in communication (Ekman & Friesen, 1969, 1975.) In various tests, where subjects have been told not to leak any emotion, then exposed to film designed to arouse emotional responses, the subjects have been surprised at how much they revealed. This research suggests that despite our intentions we will very often betray some of our real feelings in our faces and bodies.

Occasionally leakage also occurs in our verbal communication. For example, when we accidentally use the wrong word and then correct ourselves. We may think we mean the correct word, but the other word may be a more accurate reflection of how we are feeling, or what we'd really like to say. For example, when someone says 'Oh, I found it really amazing – I mean amusing', or 'just you wait till the boss – I mean your father – comes in'. More often, however, the leakage which happens in the course of verbal communication, occurs in the non-verbal aspects such as tone of voice, emphasis, appearance and so on.

Can you think of any occasions when you have noted this kind of apparent contradiction in someone else's behaviour? What were the signals which leaked the contradictory information to you?

Deliberate Leakage

Although leakage of information frequently occurs unintentionally, people sometimes use what appears to be unintentional leakage as a deliberate ploy to create the impression they want to convey. For example, a parent might say something like 'I didn't feel hurt by your behaviour' but adopt such a martyred tone or posture that the child would be almost certain to feel guilty. An apparently unintentional yawn by a student might well be a deliberate attempt to convey boredom, even if the student seemed to be showing interest in other ways. A shop assistant might be polite and attentive to a customer, but a surreptitious glance at his watch could convey – without the need for words – that he wishes the customer would hurry up and make up his mind!

> **Working with a partner, decide on a topic that you both know something about. Have a conversation on it, in the course of which one or other of you may deliberately leak information which modifies or contradicts the obvious messages of the words. Do not, however, decide beforehand who will be responsible for the leakage.**
>
> **Stop after a short time and analyse whether any leakage occured, how it occured, whether it was in fact deliberate, how it was interpreted and how you felt about doing this exercise.**

We asked how you felt about this exercise because, in our experience, people can feel self-conscious or embarrassed the first time they try an exercise of this kind. One reason is that we have a heightened awareness of the non-verbal aspects of our own and others' behaviour, and this can have an inhibiting effect at first. There is, however, evidence to show that, after sufficient practice, self-consciousness goes and what remains is an improved ability to be sensitive and receptive to non-verbal signals (Argyle, 1978a).

But there is another reason why some people feel uneasy in the particular exercise we asked you to try. By suggesting that you deliberately leak contradictory information we are, in effect, asking you to lie. Not in words, perhaps, but the intention is the same. And when you consider what we said in the previous chapter about cognitive dissonance, clearly an exercise of this kind could heighten dissonance among those who wouldn't normally lie without a very good reason! However, in spite of the ethical difficulties involved in this exercise, it does help to highlight the way that non-verbal factors can not only modify verbal statements but may even overpower the message of the words. Deliberate attempts – like the one above – to manipulate others by non-verbal means can be just as damaging to good interpersonal communication as verbal manipulation.

Perhaps you could take a few minutes to reflect upon or discuss the issues raised above before going on to the next paragraph.

Interpretation of NVC

All of the preceeding brings us back to the question of accuracy in interpreting NVC. The fact that people can recognize leakage – deliberate or otherwise – suggests, perhaps, that we all interpret NVC signals in much the same way. Whether we do or not has been the subject of considerable research over the years (Woodworth, 1938; Schlosberg, 1952; Cucelogu, 1972; Cody *et al.*, 1984). Research results suggest that some aspects of NVC seem to be fairly consistent regardless of race or culture. For example, facial expressions denoting anger, fear or distress tend to be similar in most races and are therefore fairly easy to recognize and interpret. But more subtle facial expressions, like disgust or surprise, may vary across races. The signals given by gesture or clothing are both more personal and more influenced by the culture and race of the individual. As a result there may be more variation in the way these signals are interpreted.

At this point, therefore, it might be a good idea to differentiate between the various aspects of NVC and to look at what influences our understanding and interpretation of its meaning.

Paralinguistics

Paralinguistics is the term used to describe all the vocal features which accompany our words.

These would include pitch – the rise and fall in the tone of our voices; emphasis or intonation – the way we use our voices to stress particular words and convey different meanings; the 'fillers' we use to cover hesitations while we search for the right word or think what to say next – sounds like 'er' or 'um', grunts or simply silent pauses; and the way we make changes in the pace or speed of our speech under different conditions.

Try speaking the following sentence in an even tone and with no changes in pace and no fillers:
Would you like to come round for a drink this evening?
Now try saying the same sentence, but adding fillers as indicated and speeding up the pace of the words underlined:
Would you ... er ... like to ... em ... *come round for a drink this evening?*
How did the addition of fillers and variations in pace change the meaning?
Working with a partner, if possible, try experimenting

with this, and other simple sentences, to see how many changes in meaning you can achieve simply by variations in pace, pauses or fillers. (Note, too, that people sometimes use meaningless phrases like 'you know' or 'well' to act as fillers, rather than sounds or pauses. Consider the effect these types of fillers have when used repetitively by the same speaker.)

What do you deduce from this exercise about the interpretation of this type of NVC signal?

You may have noticed that although changes in meaning are often quite subtle, they can be recognized and interpreted fairly easily by those who speak a common language. This is because we understand the conventions of our own language and can usually recognize when someone uses fillers as a result of some kind of emotion like nervousness; when they are searching for a word; when it is just a personal feature of an individual's speech; and when the fillers are being used to signal to the other people in a conversation something to the effect of 'hang on a minute, I've not finished speaking yet!'

Changes in pace which occur as a result of emotion are also fairly easy to recognize because emotions such as nervousness, or fear, or elation, etc. cause biological changes in our bodies which affect our breathing or the rate of salivation. The result is that some words may 'come out in a rush', or we have to pause more frequently to take a breath, pause, or lick our lips. As most of us will have experienced these effects ourselves we tend to be sensitive to them in other people. Even so we may sometimes make mistakes in interpretation – for example, mistaking fear or nervousness for anger or reluctance, and we may need to take account of other paralinguistic signals, together with the context of the words themselves before we can be reasonably confident that we have accurately interpreted another's meaning.

Can you think of any occasions in your own life when the pace of your speech, or the amount of fillers used was affected by your emotional state? What were the changes caused by this emotion? Did others react appropriately and appear to comprehend what you were feeling?

Pitch, Emphasis and Intonation

Although changes in pace can provide us with some information, these changes are generally accompanied by changes in pitch, emphasis or intonation which considerably add to the information available. For example, a simple sentence like 'shut the door' can convey a whole range of different meanings, depending on the rise and fall of the voice, the tone used and the words we choose to stress.

Try saying the words 'shut the door' in the ways suggested below and notice what you have to do to achieve the desired effect. (You may want to tape-record your attempts in order to analyse them afterwards.)

As a command.
As a question.
Meaning 'shut the door not the window'.
Implying disbelief.
Meaning 'don't leave the door open as you usually do.'

How many other variations in meaning can you convey with these three simple words?

You probably found that exercise fairly quick and simple to do. Whereas we had to write quite a bit in order to describe the exercise. This highlights one of the ways in which spoken and written English differ, and shows how a great deal of our verbal communication depends on quite subtle variations in paralinguistics. To convey meaning in written form we have to add punctuation such as exclamation or question marks, use typographical features like italics or underlining to indicate the stress on a word, or resort to the use of descriptive phases such as '. . . she said in disbelief' or '. . . she reproved'.

These features in written English may make it less ambiguous than spoken English. If we know the conventions of written English we find it relatively easy to understand the emotion the writer is trying to convey by her use of punctuation or descriptive phrases. It is, however, fairly easy to mistake one emotion for another when we rely on paralinguistic cues in the spoken word. This misinterpretation is often the cause of misunderstanding. Most of us are familiar with the kind of dialogue which goes something like this:

A: Would you like to go to the cinema?
B: OK.
A: You don't sound very keen.
B: What do you mean I don't sound keen? I said OK didn't I?
A: What are you getting angry about?
B: Who's angry? I'm not angry!
A: Then why are you shouting?

And so the argument goes on, with each person becoming more estranged from the other, simply because a flat, neutral tone of voice in 'OK' was interpreted as a lack of enthusiasm or agreement!

The paradox is that it is possibly our skill in *detecting* subtle nuances in intonation that creates the misunderstanding in the first place! We often have to rely on intonation to guide us as to what is meant by the words, but if we are highly sensitive to intonational changes we run the risk of reading too much into them.

In fact there is quite a bit of evidence to suggest that paralinguistic voice features lie behind many of the stereotypes that we carry about people (Rosental & Jackson, 1968). A person who speaks with a slow pace and lack of variety in intonation may be perceived by others as slow-witted. What the person has to say may therefore be regarded as unimportant. There is also a danger that if someone constantly has his utterances dismissed as stupid or unimportant the person may begin to accept that he has nothing worthwhile to say.

Paralinguistic features also affect our assessment of people from other countries, or other parts of our own country. For example, people from the north of Britain may wonder if someone from the south of England is being patronizing, when, in fact, the speech of the southerner simply carries a different intonation pattern. Similarly, the harsher and more gutteral tones of a native German speaker may, when speaking in English, sound abrupt and rather curt to English ears. The New Yorker may regard an American from one of the Southern states as lacking in enthusiasm because he uses a flat intonation pattern; the southerner may regard the New Yorker as brash or gushing because of his faster and more heavily empha- sized speech.

Consider, too, the way advertisers make use of vocal patterns in encouraging us to buy their products. Deep male voices are often employed to sell us perfume or exotic holidays, while lighter female voices beckon us to buy certain brands of chocolate or soap powder!

The effects of the different tones in male and female voices were the subject of a research study by Weitz (1979) who examined the best way to inform staff of the safety procedures to be adopted in the event of a fire. The conclusion was that the format most likely to command attention was one in which a soft female voice introduced the topic and got the audience's attention, followed by harder male tones which actually gave the crucial information.

> **Listen to a few commercials on TV and note the different ways in which advertisers use the male and female voice, variety in intonation, pace, pitch, etc. in persuading us to buy. If you have access to a video recorder you might like to record a few of these in order to analyse them more thoroughly. (You might also like to speculate on how media and advertising use of male and female voices affects our stereotypes of the male and female roles in society!)**

In studying the commercials you may have noticed that a variety of regional accents were used. This is an aspect of paralinguistics which is particularly open to misinterpretation, and one which helps reinforce stereotypes and prejudices. For example, notice how many times someone with a regional accent is used to sell mundane objects or appears in comic adverts. Advertisements for highly priced quality goods, on the other hand, are generally presented to us in what is often referred to as 'standard' or BBC English. And when the BBC itself started to employ broadcasters with 'non-standard' regional or 'ethnic' accents there was a great deal of correspondence from viewers about lowering of standards!

Regional accents can, of course, make the words themselves difficult to understand by someone from outside the region. This, in turn, may lead to increased reliance on other paralinguistic cues. But accents also carry their own intonation patterns which, as we saw above, can be misinterpreted by those with a different vocal pattern. When we combine the two we begin to see how easy it is for misunderstandings to be translated into real prejudices. A study by Macaulay & Trevelyn (1973), for example, showed that many employers within the Glasgow area were prejudiced against certain people simply because they displayed particular accents used in certain areas of the city.

> **Be as honest as you can in this exercise! Are you prejudiced against people from another race, culture or region simply because of their accent and intonation patterns? If not, why not? If you are – and we suspect that most of us suffer from at least some prejudice here – what are the particular paralinguistic features that arouse your prejudice?**

Understanding the relationship between paralinguistics and the words used – not just what we say, but the way that we say it – can help us adjust our own communication to make it easier for others to interpret accurately. For example, a study by Milot & Rosental (1967) looked at patients' willingness to undergo treatment for alcoholism. They found that the doctor's tone of voice could be a significant factor in successfully referring patients for treatment. There was a direct relationship between the use by the doctor of an angry tone of voice and lack of efffectiveness in persuading the patient. More recent research has also shown a direct link between the tone of a doctor's voice and the relationship with patients (Huntington, 1987). A warm, friendly tone encourages patients to discuss their treatment and ask questions, with the result that patients may be more likely to trust the doctor's diagnosis and carry out instructions about their treatment accurately.

Commercial and industrial firms also know that good customer relations are often dependent on the tone staff adopt in dealing with customers. For example, employees in British Rail may be asked to undertake a training programme which involves them in 'putting the customer first'. They examine 'how to speak to customers' – making the voice sound pleasant even though the message may be bad news. In other words, how to say 'your train is going to be three hours late' in such a way that passengers don't want to lynch them!

Those planning to become social workers or to take on other counselling or advisory roles in which they have to deal directly with the general public also receive training in giving appropriate para-linguistic signals, and in interpreting the signals given by others (Gibb, 1972).

Training of this kind may seem rather mechanistic and manipulative as if the whole object of the exercise were to 'con' people into believing what you want them to believe, and behaving as you want them to behave. Which brings us back to where we started – with the question of intention. If the intention is to make the customer feel better, to make the patient get better, or to help individuals to understand and relate to each other better, then we obviously have to employ the kind of communication techniques which will help us achieve our aims. If our intention is to *communicate* rather than mislead or manipulate we need to be aware of the paralinguistic features in our own and other people's speech which can both help and hinder us. As we noted earlier, we may have considerable skill in detecting subtle nuances of tone, but proper training can help us to *interpret their meaning* more accurately, and to respond appropriately.

Before going on to the next section you might like to discuss or reflect again on the ethics of NVC training and what you feel about the kind of social skills training which helps the trainee to become more sensitive in the interpretation and giving of NVC signals, and which is now fairly widely used in many professions for the training of staff in interpersonal skills with customers, clients and patients.

Facial Expression and Eye Contact

Another aspect of NVC which helps us interpret meaning is the way in which we use our eyes to regulate and control the flow of communication. If we pause in the middle of what we are saying we tend to look away from the person to whom we are speaking. This seems to act as a signal to the other person that we haven't finished and wish to say more. When we are finished we tend to look directly at the other person as much as to say 'over to you now'. Most of us are quite unaware of this regulatory mechanism until it breaks down! And we've probably all experienced the irritation of being cut off in mid-flow by someone who has not read our signals correctly, or the vaguely uncomfortable feeling we experience when someone won't look at us when we are talking (Argyle, 1978a).

If you have access to a video recorder and can work with a partner, try having a naturalistic conversation about something simple like the weather or a programme on TV. Stop

after a few minutes and play back the video slowly or frame by frame. Note the way eyes were used to perform the kind of regulatory function described above.

If you were able to do this exercise and the people involved were native Britons or Americans, you will probably have confirmed that eyes do play a regulatory part in conversation. However, unlike the facial expressions associated with emotion, the use of eye contact seems to be a less universal device. People from Eastern countries have different conventions. For example, women from certain Eastern countries are considered immodest if they look directly into a man's eyes, except under very intimate circumstances! Similarly, people of low status are not expected to look directly at those of higher status. And there is some evidence to show that even within the Western world there are variations in what is considered acceptable in terms of direct gaze during conversations (Morris, 1978).

Even though conventions in eye contact may differ, eye contact does play an important part in non-verbal communication behaviour, and is something that we learn in childhood as part of our native cultural experience. Blind people, for example, have no need to turn their heads towards someone who is speaking. But in Britain the convention of looking towards the person who is speaking is so firmly established that the blind person's behaviour can be disconcerting to the sighted, making it difficult for conversation to flow easily and naturally between them. Because of this, many schools for the blind now teach blind people to respond to this conversation by turning towards the source of speech (Hamilton, 1987). Similarly, mentally handicapped children may not pick up these conventional signals spontaneously and may have to be taught how to use their eyes effectively in communication (McClintock, 1984).

There also seems to be a close relationship between the type of eye contact used and the small head movements and gestures that occur in the course of speech. Birdwhistell (1952) found that we may be aware of head movements as small as five degrees and respond to them in our conversation. Baxter (1968) found that familiarity with the subject matter led to more frequent and pronounced gesture, and more sustained eye contact. Mortensen (1972) suggests that we can actually tell how close a relationship is between people by studying them in conversation and noting the time they spend gazing directly at each other, the similarity of their head nods and gestures and the extent to which they adopt similar postures. The less similar these behaviours, he suggests, the more likely it is that the two do not have a close personal relationship.

It is the lack of these visual signals which make some people feel awkward when holding a conversation on the telephone. A well-known writer, for example, confessed on TV that she would do anything to avoid using the telephone because it made her feel so uncomfortable. After attending communication workshops she discovered the source of her difficulty. Being a writer, she had trained herself to observe facial expressions and posture very closely and had become so dependent on these visual cues for interpreting people's meanings that she found it difficult to communicate without seeing the person face to face. It is interesting, too, that most of us continue to use expressive facial and hand movements when we talk to others on the telephone even though we know the other person can't see us.

> **Why do you think we continue to give visual signals when talking on the telephone?**
> **To find out what happens when we avoid giving visual signals, stand back to back with someone so that you can't see each other. Try to hold a simple natural conversation but try also to avoid using any kind of gesture, and try to keep your face as expressionless as you can.**
> **What happened? And how did you feel?**

Gesture

In the exercise above, the ease or difficulty you had in refraining from using gesture may very well have depended on the extent to which you normally 'talk with your hands'. This, in turn, may be determined by your nationality and your personality. Morris (1978) has shown that people from different countries not only use different gestures to accompany speech (or to replace speech), but that the amount of gesturing which is considered normal and acceptable varies across countries also. While research by Eysenk (1947) has suggested that British people who use a wide range of gesture tend to have out-going extraverted personalities.

Because of the very wide variations in gesture across individuals and nationalities, we may require to be cautious in interpreting the meaning of this aspect of NVC.

Proxemics

The study of gesture and posture is often referred to as the study of *kinesics* – the term kinesics being derived from a Greek word meaning movement. Closely linked to gesture is what has been described as proxemics.

> *Proxemics is the study of all those aspects of NVC which relate to the physical distance or proximity that exists between people in communication.*

Before going on to discuss some of the research findings here, we suggest you try the following experiments.

If you are in a room with other people, look around at how they are sitting or standing. What is the normal distance between them? Do any appear to be unusually far apart, or close together? Are any touching each other?

What do you deduce from this?

Working with a partner move towards each other until you are both in position which feels comfortable for having a conversation. Now experiment with moving closer until you are actually touching. Then try moving further away.

What did you discover in doing this exercise?

What you discovered may depend on your nationality. British people, for example, tend to feel more comfortable when they have at least two feet of space between themselves and the people to whom they are talking. If one person moves too close – invading the body space of the other – the other may become uncomfortable and stilted in conversation, unless the person close to her is either a relative or someone from the opposite sex with whom she has a strong personal relationship (Argyle, 1972).

Other nationalities may react differently. Arab men, for example tend to stand very much closer to one another than northern Europeans. Southern Europeans also tend to maintain a smaller body space between them than do the British. And what might seem like a cosy distance – *gemütlich* – to a German could seen oppressive and claustrophobic to someone from North Africa.

The extent to which we will touch one another also varies across countries. Again, the 'reserved' British and northern Europeans are less inclined towards gestures that involve touching others than are those from southern Europe, parts of America and some of the African countries.

Even so, touch does play an important part in human communication and relationships. For example, both human and animal infants who have been deprived of handling and close contact with adults in their early years can find difficulty in forming and maintaining relationships with others in later life (Harlow, 1963; Bowlby, 1952; Dobson, 1977).

Touch, too, can often be more expressive than language. In moments of extreme emotion – when words literally fail us – we often resort to using touch. A hug, a hand on the shoulder, a squeeze of the arm often say, much more clearly than words, what we are feeling for the other person at that time. Again, however, the kind of touch which is permissible here will be determined by the culture we live in and our physical relationship with the other person. And, of course, the conventions of touch extend also to our professional relationships with people like doctors, dentists and physiotherapists, and in intimate relationships within a family. What is regarded as permissible touching by a parent or a medical practitioner would be very suspect if it occurred in a lift and by a total stranger! Indeed, the behaviour of people in lifts and other confined spaces like busy trains or buses is a study in itself, and shows the lengths we may go to avoid touching and looking at other people in these situations.

The setting obviously has quite a considerable effect on the extent to which we commmunicate – or try to avoid communication; and on the combination of verbal and non-verbal behaviours we employ in the process.

Accidental touch may also have an effect on the way we perceive people. Librarians, for example, generally hand out tickets and books without touching the client. In one research study they were asked to touch – only slightly and apparently accidentally – every second person who came to return a book. Clients were then asked to fill in a questionnaire indicating their satisfaction with the quality of service provided in the library. There seemed to be some correlation between the higher levels of satisfaction expressed by those who had been touched by librarians and the lower satisfaction of those who had not (Dobson, 1982).

> **If you are attending a college or university it might be interesting to try to replicate this experiment and find out whether you obtain similar results.**
>
> **Alternatively you might like to design your own experiment to study the proxemic behaviours of people in naturalistic situations like lifts, tea-bars or pubs.**

Finally, the way we relate to and communicate with each other may also be affected by another aspect of proxemics – the way furniture and other artefacts are arranged in a room. Rather than describe the research here we leave you to make your own observations and deductions.

> **What are the features of decor and seating in a fast-food restaurant that tell you it is a fast-food place?**
>
> **How do 'better quality' restaurants create a sense of comfort and make you want to linger over a meal?**
>
> **How does it affect relationships in an interview, or in a consultation with a doctor, if the interviewer or doctor is seated behind a desk? Would changes in communication occur if the interviewer or doctor dispensed with the desk and sat alongside you?**
>
> **Have a look around your locality at the type of buildings and other street decor. What do these visual features reveal about the country, its inhabitants and the way they communicate with each other?**
>
> **Try arranging the furniture in a room in different ways and notice whether this influences the quantity and flow of communication among people using that room.**

Summary

The study of NVC is such a huge and fascinating area of communication research that we have been able to cover only the main elements of it in this chapter – paralinguistic vocal features, facial expression, gesture, dress, accent and proxemics. What we have tried to do is to show that communication between people involves far more than just the words they use, and that any communication act involves many or all of the features mentioned above.

Although communication can be regarded as a deliberate process involving the sending and receiving of messages, there are also times when communication occurs without conscious deliberate intent. Much of human communication therefore involves a process of interpretation and searching for meaning in our own and other people's behaviour and speech.

The various aspects of verbal and non-verbal communication are related to each other, making it is very difficult to 'judge' one aspect of communication in isolation.

We hope this chapter has stimulated your interest in NVC and its relationship to verbal communication. If it has, perhaps you would like to continue the debate by discussing some of the questions we leave you with:

> **Do you feel that professional training in NVC – for example in courses for nurses, social workers, etc. – can actually make those taking part more senstitve to the nuances of NVC, and therefore better communicators?**
>
> **If NVC is as important as we have been implying, should training in it be given to all professional 'communicators' and even to all pupils at school?**
>
> **What are your own feelings about NVC, and its relationship to verbal communication, after reading this chapter and trying out some of the exercises in it?**

REFERENCES

ARGYLE, M. (1978a): *Social skills at work*. Methuen

—— (1978b): *The psychology of interpersonal behaviour*. Penguin

BAXTER, J.C. (1968): Gestural behaviour during interviews. *Journal of Personality and Social Psychology*, 8, 303–7

BIRDWHISTELL, R. (1952): *Introduction to kinesics*. University of Louisville Press

BOWLBY, J. (1952): *Child care and the growth of love*. Pelican

CODY, M.J. *et al*. (1984): Deception: paralinguistic and verbal leakage. In Bostrom (ed.), *Communication yearbook no. 8*. Sage

CUCELOGU, D. (1972): Facial code in effective communication. In Speer, D.C. (ed.), *Non verbal communication*. Sage

DOBSON, C.B. (1977): *Understanding psychology*. Weidenfeld & Nicolson
—— (1982): *Attraction*. Longman

EKMAN, P. & FRIESEN, W.V. (1969): The repertoire of non-verbal behaviour. *Semiotica* 1, 49–88
—— (1975): *Unmasking the face*. Prentice Hall

EYSENK, H.J. (1947): *The dimensions of personality*. Routledge & Kegan Paul

GIBB, J.R. (1972): Non-verbal counselling. In Speers, D.C. (ed.), *Non-verbal communication*. Sage

HAMILTON, D. (1987): Private communication to authors

HARLOW, D. (1963): *Learning to love*. Albion Press

HUNTINGTON, D. (1987): *Social skills and general medical practice*. Allen & Unwin

MILOT, J. & ROSENTAL, R.A. (1967): *Experiental effects in behavioural research*. Appleton-Century Crofts

MACAULAY, M. & TREVELYN, A. (1973): *Language, social class and education*. Edinburgh University Press

McCLINTOCK, A. (1984): *Drama for mentally handicapped children*. Souvenir Press

MORRIS, D. (1978): *Manwatching*. Cape

MORTENSEN, D. (1972): *Communication*. McGraw-Hill

ROSENTAL, R.A. & JACKSON, L. (1968): *Pygmalion in the classroom*. Holt, Rinehart & Winston

SCHLOSBERG, H. (1952): The description of facial expressions. *Journal of Experimental Psychology* 44, 229–37

TANNER, D. (1986): *That's not what I mean*. Dent

WEITZ, S. (1979): *Non-verbal communication*. Oxford University Press

WOODWORTH, R.S. (1938): *Experimental psychology*. Holt

CHAPTER FOUR
LISTENING

In the previous chapter we looked at the giving of information in verbal and non-verbal communication. In this chapter we look at the receiving end of the process – listening.

It has been estimated that, of all the communication skills, listening is the one we use most and learn least about (Burley-Allen, 1982). Managers in commerce and industry spend a considerable proportion of their time in selection and appraisal interviewing, in dealing with complaints, in handling grievances and sorting out problems. All of these tasks call for highly developed listening abilities. But it is only in fairly recent years that training courses in listening skills have become recognized as a necessary part of management training.

For doctors and para-medical practitioners, listening is one of the most important elements in consultations. Again, it is only in the last 10 years or so that research has been undertaken to show the kind of listening skills necessary, and to provide training procedures in effective listening (Tuckett, 1985).

Students, too, spend much of their day in listening – as much as 75 per cent according to some surveys (Brown, 1984). And yet few will have been given any training on how to listen effectively. In fact, most people equate listening with hearing. It is assumed that if we can hear adequately, listening will present few problems. Since the majority of people *can* hear adequately, it has been assumed that all that is necessary is to ask people to listen!

Hearing and listening

There is, however, a distinct difference between hearing and listening. Hearing is a passive activity; listening is an active one. Statements like 'I'm trying to listen' or 'I am listening carefully' imply that some kind of effort is being made. Whereas hearing implies that the sound has intruded into our consciousness rather than being under our control. When we do exert control over what we hear, then we are not simply hearing, we are actively listening.

For example, think about what happens at a party. Despite all the noise and hubbub around us, most of us can deliberately tune in to one conversation and screen out much of the other noise.

Close your eyes and concentrate on all the sounds you can hear inside the room. Try to shut out all other sounds. Try to

identify the sounds you hear inside the room and decide what is the cause of them. When you are no longer aware of sounds outside, switch your attention to the sound of your own breathing and the sound of your heartbeat. If you are really listening actively you should be aware of how loud your breathing and heartbeat sound now compared to how they were at the start of the exercise.

This exercise demonstrates the difference between passive hearing and active listening, but doesn't tell us how effective our listening is.

Effective Listening

Before we can judge the effectiveness of listening we need to know what constitutes effectiveness. One group of researchers have described the process as one in which an active participator

constantly weighs up incoming information to ensure that it is coherent with information that is already available, whether that established information is derived from general background knowledge, or specific visual data or from what has previously been said. When incoming information is not consistent with already established information, the listener has to do some extra work. First, she/he must recognize that the information is inadequate or inconsistent, and secondly, she/he must identify where the inadequacy/inconsistency lies and thirdly do something about this – like checking or asking a further question. (Anderson *et al.*, 1985)

This description points to a number of important elements in the listening process – active participation, the ability to weigh up information and spot inconsistencies, and the ability to take direct action to ensure understanding.

Active Participation

We have already argued that listening is an active process. Effective listening involves even more active participation. We must, for example, be prepared to ask ourselves questions like: 'why am I listening to this?'; 'what am I hoping to find out?'; 'what's in it for me?'

If we are listening purely for entertainment purposes – as, for example, when a friend relays an interesting titbit of gossip – we may find it very easy to listen effectively. That is because we *want* to listen, we are keen to find out the news, and we can see quite clearly that what is being said is relevant to our own lives. In this situation we find it easy to maintain concentration and involvement and, because the information is likely to be presented in a simple and interesting way, we have little difficulty in understanding and remembering it.

Think back to the last TV programme you watched and enjoyed. Can you remember any of the main characters' dialogue or do you simply remember the plot? Why?

Perhaps one reason why you remembered certain aspects of plot or dialogue was because you were particularly interested in that part of the show and were able to concentrate on it without difficulty.

There are, however, many listening situations which do require more effort. For example, we may be listening in order to learn, to make judgements, to find out about a course of action, or to provide support and advice for others. In these situations we may be interested and want to listen, but it may be more difficult to do so. The speaker may be dull or using language which is difficult to understand, the information itself may seem to be boring or the ideas may be presented in such a haphazard way that it is difficult to make sense of what is being said. Under these conditions listening becomes a much more arduous task, and we may have to devise alternative strategies in order to maintain active participation.

We will look at these strategies in more detail later in the chapter, when we come to examine how listening skills can be improved. But first, let us look at some of the obstacles that can make active participation and effective listening difficult.

Jot down all the things you can think of which might prove a barrier to listening. Keep your list beside you and check how many of the barriers that we mention are on your list.

Rate of Speech

One immediate obstacle to effective listening is the mismatch between speakers' rates of talking and listeners' ability to process incoming sounds. Most people – except for auctioneers! – talk at about 150–200 words per minute. Research into what we could call 'thought rate' suggests that we can hear and process information at a much faster rate than this – something in the order of three to four times faster than that of speech production (Armstrong, 1984). When we are extremely interested in what is being said we are not conscious of this processing gap. When we are less interested it is more difficult to maintain concentration and, in the time which elapses between our primary processing and the reception of new information, we may find our attention wandering. When a speaker has a particularly slow or deliberate way of speaking, the mismatch between listening and speech rate becomes even more pronounced.

Choose two passages of text. Each should be around 250 words long. Try to find two which are of roughly the same level of difficulty. Ask a friend to read the first passage at a normal reading speed. This should take less than two minutes. Then have the second passage read to you at a much slower rate. Compare how easy or difficult it was to listen to the two and discuss how well the theory is borne out in practice.

Familiarity

Another reason for the mismatch between listening and speaking rate is the fact that we are familiar with our own language. We understand its general rules and grammatical structure, and we can often guess at what is coming next on the basis of our knowledge of the language. So we may mentally complete a sentence before the speaker has actually finished it.

On the other hand, when we are listening to a language with which we are less familiar our processing rate slows up because we find it less easy to predict with the same degree of accuracy what the next word or phrase is likely to be. That is why we tend to think that foreigners speak more quickly than we do. But research has shown that foreigners do not actually speak at a faster rate, it is simply that we listen more slowly (Ladeford & Broadbent, 1960).

This also helps to explain why students may complain that they find it difficult to listen to a lecturer because she speaks too fast. It is unlikely that the lecturer is actually speaking at much more than the normal speech rate. What is more likely is that she is using unfamiliar words and introducing new concepts which make it difficult for the listeners to predict what is coming next. Hence their processing rate slows and they may have to use up additional processing time in trying to work out the meaning of new words and ideas before attending to and processing the next bit of incoming information.

Structure

Research has also shown that, in processing incoming information, we tend to wait for a natural grammatical break in the speech and then process the previous part in one, fairly large, grammatical chunk (Garrett *et al.*, 1966). If a speaker pauses or hesitates in a part of a sentence that would not normally indicate a comma or full stop, we tend to wait for the next grammatical break before processing the information. If, however, a speaker is very hesitant we may find it difficult to maintain concentration long enough to wait for the grammatical break and may abandon our attempt to process that piece of information. The result will be that we forget what has been said or simply fail to understand it.

Ask a friend to read a passage of about 250 words but to do so in a hesitant way, stopping at points where there would not normally be a grammatical pause. Discuss how easy it was to listen and how much sense you made of the passage.

Attention Span

Another problem can be the extent of the human attention span. Attention span refers to the amount of time that one can attend to incoming information; how long one can listen without becoming tired and losing concentration.

Research has shown that most people can maintain a high level of listening concentration for around 15–20 minutes (Bligh, 1983). After this time concentration becomes more difficult because our attention span tends to operate in a 'rise – fall – rise' pattern – with periods of concentrated listening alternating with drops in concentration which allow us to rest before resuming concentrated listening once more.

Bligh found that it imposes a severe strain on students when they have to try to maintain their concentration throughout lectures which consist of 50–60 minutes of solid talk by one speaker. At the start the speaker's voice represents a fresh stimulus. Arousal is high and attention is easy. As the speaker's voice and patterns of intonation become more familiar it becomes more difficult to attend. If, however, the lecturer stops speaking occasionally and writes on the board, switches on an overhead projector or introduces some other audio-visual aid, these act as a new stimulus which reactivate the attention and increase concentration.

Similarly, when a speaker tells a joke he often uses a different pattern of intonation to the one he uses for giving information. This is why we often find it easier to maintain concentration and to listen more effectively to a speaker who enlivens his talk with a bit of humour. Variety in a speaker's pace, pitch and intonation will also make it easier for listeners to increase their attention span as will the occasional effective pause.

Memory Span

Closely related to attention span is what we might call 'memory span'. Most psychologists nowadays accept that human beings have at least two types of memory – short and long term. Incoming information goes directly into our short-term memory store. Short-term memory has a limited capacity and information held in short-term memory is very easy to forget. The information held in short-term memory, therefore, needs to be transferred to long-term memory, which operates rather like an efficient data storage system. As new information comes in it is filed under an appropriate heading and cross-referenced to other related categories of information.

Obviously, this cross-referencing happens very quickly and sometimes, if we don't listen properly, we mis-hear information, store it in the wrong file and find it very difficult to gain access to it at a later stage. We haven't actually forgotten – we just don't know how to gain access to the memory! Similarly, when we hear new information which doesn't 'fit' into any of our existing category systems we may take longer to hear and process the information because it is as if we have to take the time to open and label a new file before we can take in any more information about the subject. This is why we said earlier that it is much easier to listen to information which is in a familiar language, and why we find it more difficult to listen effectively when we are being introduced to new concepts and ideas.

Although a great deal of research has gone into the human memory process, psychologists are still not completely sure of the mechanisms which govern this processing and transfer of information from short- to long-term memory. What we do know from their research is that information to which we have not paid conscious attention is unlikely to be transferred efficiently. We also know that it is almost always the middle portion of a message that is least well remembered (Mortensen, 1972).

> **Ask someone to read you out a long telephone number. You may be able to remember it accurately as soon as you have heard it. But if you do not write it down or repeat it over to yourself you are unlikely to remember it after quite a short period of time. If the number is very long you may forget some of it almost as soon as you have heard it. Try this a few times and note how many numbers you remember accurately after one hearing.**

Most people can remember numbers of seven or eight digits quite easily and accurately. With longer numbers there is a tendency to remember the first and the last few digits, and to forget or mix up the numbers in between. One reason for this relates directly to the rise–fall–rise pattern of our attention span. The close attention paid to the first part of any message tends to ensure that it is remembered. The last part is remembered because it is the part most recently heard and there is no further incoming information to compete with it for processing. We remember less of the middle portion because we have listened to it less attentively and because it has to compete for processing time with both the information which has gone before and the information which follows it.

Motivation

All of the obstacles to listening which we have looked at so far are directly related to our physical ability to attend to and process information. There are, however, a number of psychological factors which also determine how effectively we are able to listen on any occasion.

We have already hinted at one of these – motivation. If we are really interested in something, and strongly motivated to listen to a particular piece of information, we may be able to overcome many of the physical barriers to listening. We will be less conscious of the processing gap between speaking and listening rates; we will tend to maintain a somewhat longer attention span or to find ways of increasing our concentration when it starts to flag; and, because we are attending more closely, we may remember more of the information presented. Of course, the opposite also applies! This is why we suggested earlier in the chapter that to be an effective listener one needs to ask *why* one is listening and 'what's in it for me?'

Attitudes

Attitudes, too, can affect how well we listen. Just as attitudes can interfere with our ability to make impartial judgement and alter the way we perceive people, so people with different attitudes, listening to the same message, will tend to 'hear' the message differently!

> **Record about five minutes of a speech by a leading politician. Then play it back to people whom you know to be either strongly in favour of or strongly against that politician's party. After they've listened to the passage, ask them to write down as much as they can remember of what was said – using the speaker's actual words if they can remember them. You should find it interesting to compare the two versions and to see how attitudes and prejudices show up in what is or isn't remembered, and in the subtle changes made in the wording. (By the way, if one of your friends can write down the passage word for word after only one hearing, this may not tell you much about her attitudes, but it will show that she's one of those rare people who have an exact aural memory! You might find it interesting to speculate on the effects there might be on interpersonal communication if everyone had a memory of this kind!)**

Since most of us do not have this type of photographic memory we have to guard against this tendency to listen selectively when faced with a speaker whose viewpoint opposes our own. Selective listening can also occur if something in the speaker's voice, accent, clothes or make-up triggers off a particular prejudice. When this happens the listener may start thinking about something related to that prejudice; or mentally rehearsing the arguments that might be used to counter what the speaker is saying; or simply spend the time in becoming annoyed at the speaker. As a result the listener stops attending and may very well miss much of what has been said.

Fake Listening

Another rather curious way in which attitude can affect the listening process is how some people react when they don't want to listen. They assume that what they are going to hear will be less interesting than the thoughts in their own heads and decide to go on thinking their own thoughts regardless of what the speaker says. However, it can often be hurtful or impolite to the speaker to show that we aren't listening. We may not want to hurt the person's feelings, or incur their wrath. So some people have perfected the technique of 'fake' listening. They look alert, they give the occasional nod, or smile, or word of encouragement which leads the speaker to believe that they are listening intently to what is being said. In fact they are miles away in some daydream of their own!

What is interesting about this is that it is actually very difficult to do. If someone has managed to perfect this technique they have the potential to be a very good listener because the amount of concentration required to maintain an alert façade while not listening is at least as great as that required to listen attentively!

> For this exercise you will need at least three people – a speaker, a listener and one or more observers. It would also be useful to tape record the exercise so that you can check back on the accuracy of the listener's recall.
>
> In the first part of the exercise the speaker talks for a couple of minutes about something that interests him. While he speaks the listener should try to listen as intently as possible, and to show the speaker that he is listening.
>
> The observer should take careful note of the ways in which the listener conveys to the speaker that he is listening. The listener then notes down as much as he can remember of what was said.
>
> Repeat the exercise using a different topic of conversation. This time the listener tries to give the impression of listening but what he is actually doing is mentally trying to repeat the alphabet backwards. Again the observer notes the listener's reactions, and when the speaker has finished the listener jots down what he can remember.
>
> Discuss the observer's findings, and the feelings of both the listener and the speaker about the exercise itself.

Other Distractions

Finally, there are the other, more obvious barriers that can hamper us when we try to listen – a warm stuffy room that makes us want to drift off into sleep or daydreams; an environment that is so noisy that it's almost impossible to hear what's being said; disturbances outside the room that are very difficult to ignore; seats so uncomfortable that after a while we can think of nothing else; and so on. Fortunately, these barriers are relatively easy to overcome in most cases, and, with just a little foresight or planning, we can at least create an environment that makes it possible, rather than impossible to listen!

Improving Listening Ability

Now that we've looked at the many obstacles to listening we should be in a much better position to understand the listening process, and that, in itself, is one stage towards improving effectiveness. For example, look back at some of the exercises we have already suggested in this chapter. These provide a practical method of testing theories, but they can also be used to help you recognize the barriers to listening and, by practising the exercises, to learn to overcome these barriers.

By learning to focus attention on your breathing, for example, you are training yourself to concentrate on a specific sound stimulus. With just a few minutes of regular practice over a period of a few days you will find that you can quickly reach the stage when you can shut out distractions and concentrate on hearing the sound of your own breathing even in a very noisy environment. When you reach this stage you can then try focusing on other sounds. Before long your general ability to concentrate will improve and, with it, your ability to listen actively whenever you wish to do so.

Similarly, since you know that you are liable to forget – or stop attending – to the middle portion of a message, you can practice memory exercises in which you make a conscious effort to remember the middle portion. At first this may have the effect of causing you to remember the first and last parts less well because you will have substituted a 'fall–rise–fall' pattern for the normal 'rise–fall–rise' attention pattern. With practice, however, you should find that you can gradually extend your concentration span to cover more of the message, with a consequent increase in the amount remembered.

By practising listening to material being read in a variety of styles – quickly, slowly, hesitantly, in an unfamiliar accent, etc. – you can learn to ignore the rate and style of speech and to concentrate instead on the formation being presented. As your concentration improves there may be an added bonus. Improved concentration makes listening easier, easier listening reduces mental and physical tiredness and, even more importantly, helps us remain motivated to continue listening. This, in turn, may increase our attention span and, consequently, the amount of information remembered.

Listening – A Two-Way Process

Listening is a two-way process. It depends not only on the listener's ability to overcome barriers to listening, it also depends on the speaker's ability to make himself understood. As we saw in the exercise on fake listening, a listener can give feedback signals to the speaker which suggest that her message is being 'received and understood' even when it isn't. Under normal circumstances, however, most listeners do not set out to deceive in this way. When they cease to listen actively they often show signs of it in their posture, or their facial expression, or in the fact that they become restless. Lack of understanding is often shown in a puzzled look or a quick frown. The good speaker will take note of these feedback signals – will rephrase or repeat what she has been saying, will ask the listener if she understands, or will introduce a new stimulus to regain the listener's attention. In this way the speaker is making it easier for the listener and the 'dialogue' between them becomes much more satisfying for both parties.

> **Working in pairs, one partner gives the other directions on how to get from one place to another. Do not use hand gestures to supplement speech, and give the information in as boring a voice as possible. The listener may not interrupt until the instructions are complete. The listener then tries to repeat back what she has heard.**
>
> **Change partners and repeat the exercise, only this time the listener may interrupt to ask for clarification if necessary, the speaker may use gesture to supplement speech, and should speak with a naturally varied voice. Again the listener should try to repeat back what she has heard.**
>
> **Compare the listener's performation in the two situations and analyse the results.**

Unfortunately, there are some speakers who are so nervous, or so intent on their part in the process, that they seem to be oblivious of the feedback listeners give. They carry on regardless of how bored or restless their audience becomes, and simply ignore any signs of puzzlement or lack of understanding. When faced with a speaker like this, the motivation of the listeners becomes of paramount importance.

We've already argued that you can increase motivation by knowing why you are listening and what you want to get out of it. Another way of maintaining motivation is to set yourself a challenge. Make it a matter of pride to be able to listen actively regardless of the quality of the speaker, and test yourself afterwards to see how well you succeeded. At first you may not succeed particularly well, but, with practice, you should find yourself becoming more adept. And eventually you should be able to reach the stage when you can maintain at least some interest even when the speaker is doing her best to make it hard for you!

Cobwebs and Topic Maps

Many people find that taking notes during a talk or lecture not only helps them record and remember the content but also helps them maintain an interest in what is being said. Some students find a 'cobweb' approach useful here. In this method the main point of the lecture is put in the centre of the page and, as the lecture proceeds, additional material is added as shown in the figure below.

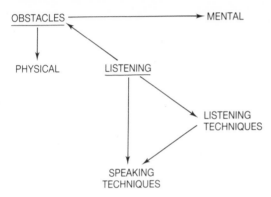

Fig 4.1

The advantage of this method is that it allows us to jot down the main points, and the relationships between them without having to write so much that we might be distracted from listening.

One researcher (Pask, 1976) has suggested that if students draw out topic maps of the areas to be covered in lectures they achieve a better understanding of theoretical material than those who do not. A topic map is a bit like a sightseeing guide, allowing us to check out the main points of interest before we set out on a journey. So, if we know in advance what the general subject of the lecture is going to be, we can check out the booklist and draw up a list of topic headings with, perhaps, some indication of the questions we want answered or the kind of information we hope to obtain about the various areas. We can also try to get some idea of how the various aspects of the subject relate to each other – what are the routes that connect one point with another? As the lecturer moves from point to point we can slot the information in under the headings we have already created, and create new headings only for those items which are unfamiliar or unexpected.

By drawing up topic maps or cobwebs we can increase our awareness of what we are listening for, and active participation is likely to
be increased as a direct result. Similarly, the preparation involved in
drawing out topic maps can make all the difference between listening
to a lecture in which everything is new and difficult to understand,
and one in which we can at least recognize some familiar landmarks
and use these as a guide to help us process and understand the rest of
the talk.

Other research has shown that an appreciation of the structure in a
talk can help both the speaker and the listener (Brown, 1982).
Knowing how to build up a talk can, in itself, make it easier to listen
more effectively to other people's talks. It helps us recognize the
distinction between main points which have to be recorded, minor
points which are of less significance, and other features such as
examples and asides which may simply act as illustration or
reinforcement of the main ideas being put forward. This, in turn,
helps us to weigh up the significance of the information, makes it
easier to take notes and encourages us to listen for ideas and
concepts rather than simply trying to remember facts.

For this exercise you should work with a partner, and you
will need a tape recorder to verify your score.

Your partner is going to describe a game, a hobby or some
activity in which he is interested. In doing so he will give a
number of important facts, and also his ideas and opinions
about the topic. As you listen, note down the important facts
using either a list or the cobweb form described in the
chapter. Do not include opinions or examples – only facts.
Tape record your partner. When he has finished, use your
facts as a guide to giving a full report of what was said,
including any opinions or ideas you remember. Tape record
your summary, so that you can compare the two versions
and see how similar or otherwise they were.

When you've finished ask yourself the following questions:

• Is it easier to listen for facts or opinions or ideas?
• When you note down facts does this help you remember
the other aspects of what was said?
• When you listen only for facts how do you judge which
facts are the most important ones?
• Does taking a note of facts help you remember the other
information given by the speaker?

Change partners and try the same exercise again, only this
time the listener is listening for the most significant points
that the speaker makes, whether these be ideas, facts,
opinions, examples or any other type of information. Note

down only the points which you consider to be significant and, if you wish, indicate whether they were facts, opinions, etc. At the end of the exercise the listener will summarize as before.

Consider whether the answers to any of the questions above would be different after this part of the exercise, and discuss with your partner whether the listener did, in fact, pick up all the points that the speaker thought were important.

Improving Listening in Interview Situations

Most of the listening techniques we've looked at so far have been aimed mainly at the skills required for listening to lectures, public talks and discussions. At the start of the chapter, however, we mentioned a variety of listening situations: counselling, consultation, negotiation, etc. What all of these have in common is that they involve an interview between two or more people.

The listening skills involved in interviews are somewhat different from those required for listening to lectures. To begin with, the interview situation is much more of an active dialogue between the participants, with both alternating between the roles of listener and speaker. Neither party is likely to speak for very long at any one time. There may be occasions when the speaker is not so much trying to express and clarify a viewpoint, as to conceal his true feelings or to create a particular impression. The outcome of the interview may be important to either or both parties, so both may be motivated to listen actively. The dialogue which takes place in their discussion is unlikely to be repeated on another occasion so each person may need to be sure that he has heard and understood what the other is saying and that each has had a chance to say what he means or wants to say.

Obviously, the techniques of concentration and recall which we mentioned earlier are important in this situation. The feedback signals are even more important, since the effective listener in an interview will 'listen with his eyes' as much as his ears in order to detect whether the speaker is saying all that he wants to say or whether he is ill-at-ease or worried. Both need to take account of these feedback signals, and to be able to ask the right questions that will make for understanding. This is particularly important in a medical, counselling or job interview, and in negotiations where lack of understanding could have serious consequences.

Also very important in an interview is the part played by stereotyped attitudes and prejudices. In job selection, for example, an interviewer who is prejudiced against a particular style of dress, or a racial or cultural group, may not only fail to 'hear' accurately what the candidate is saying, he may also respond with questions which make it almost impossible for the candidate to do himself justice. At the other end of the spectrum there is the interviewer who fails to listen because he is more interested in his own opinions than in what the other has to say.

Later in the book (Chapter Nine) we will be looking in more detail at the interview process. In the context of listening, however, there is a particular technique which not only works well in interview, but also helps reduce the effects of prejudice. The technique is that of 'reflecting back'.

Reflecting Back

In one experiment a number of volunteers were divided into two groups. The first group were assigned to a counsellor, who interviewed them about a problem they had. The second group worked through a computer diagnosis session in which they punched information into the computer and the computer responded with questions. In general, those who had worked with the computer felt more satisfied with the outcome! When the reasons for this were analysed, the experimenters found that the computers were seen to 'listen better', to be better at spotting the 'real problem' and less inclined to interrupt with trivial questions or impose their own views. Further analysis showed that, whereas the human counsellors felt that they had to offer advice, the computers simply reflected back the problem to the clients by searching out the key words and responding appropriately (Huntington, 1987).

If the client punched in a statement like 'I have a problem with my daughter, Mary', the computer would respond with 'I'm sorry to hear you have a problem with Mary. What seems to be the trouble?' If the client then punched in 'She's so rude and completely out of control', the computer would respond with something like 'I'm sorry you feel that way. Why do you think that is?'

The human volunteers felt that they had to get the details and would perhaps interrupt with questions like 'And how old is Mary?' or 'Is she an only child?' These questions may have been relevant in the general context of problem solving but, to the clients, they suggested that the counsellor had preconceived ideas, did not really want to listen to what they had to say, or changed the flow of the conversation making it difficult to keep to the main point.

The other important point here is that the clients had to type in the information and so they tried to use as few words as possible in order to get the real message across.

We're not suggesting that human beings should be replaced by computers! In fact, good teachers have been using this technique since the time of Socrates and it was human beings, after all, who programmed the computers successfully. But what this experiment can teach us is the need for speakers to think carefully about what they want to say, and the need for listeners to be alert to the key points and to respond with words that show they have listened to what the speaker said, rather than with what they think *they* ought to be saying to comfort, advise or instruct the speaker. By using this 'reflecting back' technique, listeners not only develop very real abilities to spot the important points in a mass of detail, they also ensure that they attend more closely and remain active participants in the listening process, rather than mentally rehearsing what they should say next.

> **Get a partner to describe a problem. Listen carefully, and only interrupt when necessary in order to 'reflect back' a question to the speaker. At the end of the interview, discuss with your partner how it felt, how successful you were, and whether the main points which he or she wanted to discuss were properly dealt with. If the session was successful, why was that? If it was unsatisfactory, what were the reasons?**

As a final exercise, read through the pieces of dialogue given below and try to work out which aspect of the listening process is illustrated in each.

> **Speaker: So getting to the library is a real problem.**
> **Listener: Yes it must be. Have you tried asking some of the others to collect your books for you?**

> **Speaker: So getting to the library is a real problem.**
> **Listener: Oh, I wouldn't worry about it. Students always seem to make more of their problems. And none of the students seem to read much anyway. In any case the library is open late on a Wednesday.**

> **Speaker: So it's really awkward for me, what with not getting to train, and no car, and having this Saturday job I just don't know what to do. But I don't want to miss playing in the team now that I've got the chance.**
> **Listener: Funny you should be sitting there saying that. Do you know who was sitting in that seat last night? Fred Jones. He's doing really well for himself. Gone into partnership with his father and seems to be making a mint.... He was telling me all about it. He said....**

Summary

To sum up, here again are the main points we have dealt with in this chapter:

1 Listening is a two-way process involving the giving and receiving of information. Speakers and listeners have to take equal responsibility for ensuring that the process is an effective one.

2 It is easier to listen when the environment is a suitable one, so care should be taken to ensure that physical factors such as temperature, comfort, noise, etc., are as well controlled as possible. It may not be possible to control other obstacles such as rate of speech or familiarity of material, but at least it is possible to be aware of their potential effects.

3 Active processing – i.e. trying always to relate new information to existing ideas and categories of information that we already have stored in our minds – is a necessary part of effective listening. It aids recall and helps reduce the extent of forgetting.

4 Active participation is made easier if the listener is motivated to listen, knows why he is listening and what he hopes to get out of it.

5 Attention tends to operate in a 'rise–fall–rise' pattern. Being alert to this may help us maintain attention in the difficult middle section of a listening situation.

6 Attention and memory are closely linked. Exercises which improve concentration may also help memory, but specific memory exercises can help increase both our attention and memory span.

7 When listening to lectures or talks, one way of ensuring that information is efficiently processed and transferred from short- to long-term memory is to take notes based on the 'cobweb' or topic map approaches. This also helps increase active participation in the listening process.

8 It may not always be possible for speakers to use language or concepts which are familiar to the listeners, but speakers can help listeners by speaking more slowly when introducing new concepts. Speakers should also look for feedback signals and react appropriately when using words which may not be familiar to their audience. The good listener will make it easier for the speaker by showing that he is attending, and by giving appropriate verbal or non-verbal signals when he fails to understand.

9 The good listener will be wary of trying to fake attention – it can become a habit!

10 In an interview situation it is necessary to guard against prejudice or the tendency to dominate the conversation. The technique of 'reflecting back' helps the listener to maintain active participation and clarify the speaker's views.

REFERENCES

ANDERSON, A., BROWN, G. & YULE, G. (1985): *A report to Scottish Education Department: An investigation of listening comprehension skills.* Scottish Education Department

ARMSTRONG, S.L. (1984): What some concepts might not be. *Cognition* 13, 263–308

BLIGH, D. (1983): *What's the use of lectures?* Penguin

BROWN, G. (1982): *Explaining and lecturing.* Methuen

BURLEY-ALLEN, D. (1982): *Listening, the forgotten skill.* Wiley

FODER, J.A., BEVER, T.G. & GARRETT, M.F. (1974): *The psychology of language.* McGraw-Hill

HUNTINGTON. D. (1987): *Social skills and general medical practice.* Allen & Unwin

LADEFORD, P. & BROADBENT, D. (1960): Perception of sequence in auditory events. *Journal of Experimental Psychology* 12, 162–70

MORTENSEN, C.D. (1972): *Communication.* McGraw-Hill

PASK, G. (1976): Styles and strategies of learning. *British Journal of Educational Psychology* 46, 128–48

TUCKETT, D. (1985): *Meetings between experts.* Tavistock

CHAPTER FIVE
COMMUNICATION MODELS

If you've worked through this book from the beginning you will have read several thousand words. How much simpler it would be, for authors and readers alike, if there was one clear diagram which could describe and explain the processes of communication and avoid the need for lengthy verbal explanations! Unfortunately no one has yet come up with such a diagram, although over the past 40 years there has been considerable interest among communication specialists in attempting to do so.

These diagrams are generally referred to as *communication models*. All models – whether they be computer-generated simulations, scaled-down working models of a piece of machinery, maps, flow-charts, or diagramatic representations – share the same basic purposes. First, they seek to capture all the essential features of a real situation in a simplified form which allows it to be described, explained and understood more easily. Secondly, they allow us to manipulate some of the aspects of the situation in order to predict what might happen if these aspects were changed. And finally, we can use the information provided by the model to test out theories, to find out whether they might work in practice and to stimulate further research.

Communication models may attempt to describe a particular theory, a process or part of a process, or a single communication event. Even the most complex models are likely to contain some simplification. The very simple models allow us to focus attention on specific factors rather than having to cope with all the complex interactions of human communication at the one time. Some of these simple models are based on quite complex theories of communication, and each of these theories has added to our understanding. More importantly, the theories underlying the models have a practical use in that they enable us to pinpoint some of the factors which can help us to communicate more effectively in practice.

In this chapter we examine three of these models and discuss the different theories of communication which they represent. But before going on to look at the models produced by professional theorists, let's look at three produced by non-specialists – in this case students who were studying communication as part of a more general business studies course. Each of the models attempts to describe and explain the processes that were occurring during two minutes of a communication class.

P R O C E S S

Fig 5.1 Model 1

Model 1 is probably more of a cartoon than a diagram but we feel that it does describe quite effectively the communication – or perhaps lack of communication – that was taking place.

Look again at Model 1. What does it tell you about the processes that were occurring? Can you pinpoint any aspects of communication theory which have been dealt with in the previous chapters which are included in the model? If you are working on your own, jot these down so you can refer to them later in the chapter. If you are working with others, compare your understanding of the model with that of others in your group.

The next model is more diagramatic and takes the form of a flow-chart.

Try to work out what communication processes Model 2 describes or explains. How effective is it as a model?

Those of you who are familiar with flow-charts may have noticed that Model 2 represents a very odd communication situation. If we follow any of the arrows leading out to the right we find ourselves stuck in a discussion box with no way out! But if we follow the downward arrows only we cut out any possibility that discussion occurred! The student assures us that this was not his intended

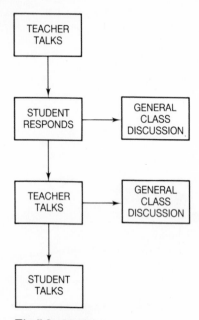

Fig 5.2   Model 2

meaning. What he was trying to describe was a relatively structured teaching situation in which there was some one-way communication from teacher to class but with opportunities for two-way discussion of the points being dealt with.

> **Can you improve on Model 2 in order to make it a more accurate representation of the teaching situation described above?**

The final model represents the simplest of the diagrams produced by the students in this class.

TEACHER ——————► CLASS ——————► TEACHER

Fig 5.3   Model 3

> **What does Model 3 tell you about the communication processes occurring in the lesson?**

Model 3 is, in fact, an adaptation of a well-known professionally developed model of communication – that produced by Shannon and Weaver in the late 1940s.

The Shannon and Weaver Model

Shannon and Weaver were two electronic engineers working for the Bell Telephone Company. Much of the terminology they use has been borrowed from electronic communication systems theory and applied to human communication. Like Model 3 above, the Shannon and Weaver model assumes that communication is a linear process in which a message is sent directly and intentionally via a transmitter(T) to a receiver(R) and is picked up and understood by the recipient of the message. In its most basic form the model can be represented as shown in the diagram below:

| S | T | R | D |
| SOURCE | TRANSMITTER | RECEIVER | DESTINATION |

Fig 5.4   The Shannon and Weaver Model

Because this model focuses on the process of transmission of information, rather than on the content of the information being sent, it is often referred to as a transmission or process model. Many subsequent theorists have accepted that the transmission process is one of the most vital elements in communication and this has given rise to a whole school of thought in communication which starts with the basic premise that if the information does not get through accurately and with minimum distortion from transmitter to receiver, then little communication can take place. Later in the chapter we will look at another view of communication which challenges this premise, but, for the moment, let us look more closely at the Shannon and Weaver model.

In this model the terms transmitter and receiver refer to the instruments used in the process of transmission – for example, the human voice and ear, the telephone, letters sent by post, etc. As engineers, however, Shannon and Weaver were aware that a message hasn't much chance of being picked up by the receiver and reaching its intended destination unless both receiver and transmitter are using compatible *channels of communication* and the same *method of coding and decoding* the message.

Channel of communication refers to the physical method by which the information is transmitted and received – light waves, sound waves, physical gestures, etc.

Coding, or *encoding*, means putting the message to be sent into a form that is compatible with the channel of communication used.

For example, a message transmitted by means of a letter will use the postal service as the channel of communication and the code will be that of the written word. If the channel for transmission is sound transmitted by the human voice then, obviously, the code is the spoken word, together with all the paralinguistic codes that accompany it.

How many channels of communication can you jot down in one minute?

What would be appropriate codes for each?

Clearly, the recipient must also be using a receiver and a channel of communication that is compatible with that used by the transmitter. There's not much point in sitting waiting for the telephone to ring if the message has been sent by post! And, of course, the recipient must be capable of decoding the message if the information is to get through. A telephone call in Japanese to a person who speaks only English is likely to be an unproductive communication exercise!

If we include these additional elements the more expanded form of the model would look like this:`

S ——— ENCODES ———→ T ——————→ R ——— DECODES ———→ D
                        COMMUNICATION CHANNEL

Fig 5.5

The assumptions built into this model are that communication flows directly from source to destination, that the message sent is determined by the source and that, assuming there are no blockages or distortions to stop the message getting through, the message received at its destination will be the same message as that sent.

From their work on electronics, however, Shannon and Weaver were very aware of how static electricity or 'noise' could interfere with the electrical transmission process, resulting in distortion of the message. They felt that the concept of 'noise' was a useful one to incorporate into their model in order to represent anything which interfered with reception and presented a barrier to effective communication. Expanded to include the concept of noise the model would look like this:

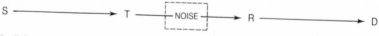

Fig 5.6

Look back at Model 1 on page 69. What are the noise factors in the model which are preventing effective transmission of the message from teacher to class?

How many barriers to communication did you note down when you originally looked at the model?

Who is the transmitter? Who are the receivers? What channels of communication are being used?

What channels of communication and methods of encoding are you using as you try to understand the messages contained in the model?

From your study of earlier chapters in this book can you identify any other perceptual, attitudinal, verbal or non-verbal factors which could interfere with the TR process and be classed as noise in the Shannon and Weaver model?

Channel Overload

So far we have dealt directly with the aspects of communication contained within the model. But, as a result of producing their model, Shannon and Weaver became aware of a number of other aspects of communication which may be inferred from the model, but which are not directly included in it. For example, the concept of channel overload – literally too many signals being sent out at the same time resulting in the channel being overloaded and unable to cope effectively with the messages sent.

An obvious example of channel overload is what happens when you find yourself in a situation where you are trying to listen to several people who are all talking to you at once. Because the human ear has a relatively limited capacity as a reception channel for sound waves, it becomes difficult, if not impossible, to hear and respond to what anyone is saying unless one screens out some of the speakers and listens selectively to only one. Channel overload, therefore, represents another potential source of noise in the transmission process.

Can you think up other examples of channel overload?

If you are working by yourself try this test to find out just how much information you can pick up when faced with a channel overload situation. Switch on the radio, the TV, a cassette recorder, and any other 'noisemakers' you have available in one room. If possible tune your equipment to programmes which contain the spoken word, then note how much or little you manage to catch of the various messages coming at you. You might also like to work out, from your reading of the earlier chapters in this book, why you were able to receive what you did receive and whether you made any conscious choices in doing so.

If you are working with a group, a much simpler method is for everyone to talk to one person at once!

Redundancy

When dealing with electronic or mechanical methods of information transmission one way of avoiding channel overload is to ensure that there are sufficient channels available at any time to cope with the amount of signals being sent out. When only a small number of signals are being sent out several of these channels will be unnecessary and unused but they will be available to be brought into use if required. If we build enough unnecessary or *redundant* channels into the system we should, in theory, ensure that channel overload will never occur and thus increase the probability that the message transmitted will be received.

The idea that adding redundant channels would increase the probability of the signal getting through, led Shannon and Weaver on to theorize that the amount of *redundancy* which was built into a communication system could be regarded as a *measure of probability* of whether the transmitted signal would be received and decoded easily and accurately. If, for example, we increase the strength or clarity of a signal beyond the level that is strictly necessary the extra strength or clarity may be redundant but it does increase the possibility that the signal will get through.

Similarly, if we send out the same information simultaneously via a number of different channels we increase the probability that the message will get through on one of them. Thus advertisers, for example, may use press, TV, billboards and cinema to send out the same message about their product and to increase the probability that consumers will get the message. Alternatively, advertisers may include in their advertisements a whole range of symbols, all of which send out the same basic message. Even if some of these symbols are missed, the fact that there are so many signals all containing the same information increases the likelihood that the message will be received and understood.

> **Look at the advertisement opposite. Work out how many ways there are in which the advertiser has repeated the same message. Is there anything in the advertisement which seems out of keeping with the rest of the information? If you didn't have the words to tell you what the product is, how easy would it be to guess at it from the other information given?**

Most people would probably agree that this advert contains so many signals, all giving out the same information, that it would be difficult to make a mistake about the product even without the words. Moreover, there is nothing in the advert which is out of keeping with the overall message – nothing unexpected which causes us difficulty in working out what the message is. The advertisers have built in so much additional or redundant information that this advert is easy to decode. Even without the words there are a limited number of choices open to us in deciding what the product is and this also increases the probability that the message will get through.

Only one decaffeinated coffee has that golden roasted taste.

We only select from the world's finest coffee beans.
These select beans are naturally decaffeinated and are
then blended and golden roasted to capture the rich,
smooth taste of the perfect cup of coffee.

'Nescafé Gold Blend'

'Nescafé' and 'Gold Blend' are registered trade marks
to designate Nestlés instant coffees.

See how quickly you can fill in the missing words in the following sentences:

Jack and —— went up the hill.

Mary —— a little lamb.

Old King Cole was a —— old soul.

We suspect that anyone familiar with British nursery rhymes could fill in the blanks in a few seconds. The missing words here are so predictable, so expected, that we don't have to think about choosing a word. We simply decode the message automatically. In this context the missing words are redundant – so predictable that they become unnecessary in decoding the message. Redundancy, therefore, can be regarded not simply as additional channels, or additional messages, but also as information which is so predictable that we are unlikely to have any difficulty in decoding it, even when there is some distortion in it – as, in this case, words missing. The use of familiar, expected signals increases the probability that the message will be easy to decode accurately.

However, as we discovered in our study of perception, we also know that when a signal becomes too predictable and too familiar it may well be disregarded. It carries no new information and may safely be ignored. Thus, while a certain amount of redundancy in a signal will increase the possibility that it will be received and understood, the inclusion of too much redundancy may have the opposite effect of encouraging us to disregard much – or even all – of the message sent.

Phatic Communication

Another theorist, Jakobson, has argued that the most predictable forms of communication – for example, the conventional forms of greeting such as 'good morning', 'how are you?' and, in Britain, observations about the weather – are redundant in the sense that they convey no information through the words. What they can do is perform a social function, opening or keeping open the channels of communication between individuals. We may feel it is inappropriate at a given moment to engage in a deep meaningful conversation with someone but that it is important to acknowledge their presence and show some kind of goodwill towards them. It is under these circumstances that we employ the conventional social rituals accepted in our culture. Jakobson has called this form of redundancy *phatic communication*.

Entropy

Another concept borrowed from physics and applied rather differently by Shannon and Weaver to human communication is that of entropy. In physics entropy is a measure of the disorder within any system. The greater the degree of disorder the higher the entropy. In communication theory the term entropy has been used to describe information which is unpredictable and unexpected in the context in which it is found. 'Mary had a little lamb' is predictable in the context of nursey rhymes. 'Mary had a little kangaroo' is rather less so. In communication terms it is more entropic.

If a degree of redundancy or predictability in communication increases the possibility that a message will be easily decoded, the use of entropy has the opposite effect. When faced with information which is entropic, there are more choices open to us in deciding how to decode the message. Because there are more choices available the information will be more difficult to decode and there is more chance that we will decode it in a different way from that intended by the sender of the message.

Consider the following conversation:

A: Morning.
B: Morning.
A: Nice day, isn't it?
B: Yes.

All highly predictable, easy to decode and, perhaps, boring – unless one accepts that it represents an example of the phatic communication described above.

Now consider this conversation:

A: Morning.
B: Morning.
A: Nice day, isn't it?
B: For a murder!

The last line here is entropic – unexpected, unpredictable and difficult to decode. Is B making a joke? Is he a sinister character about to carry out a threat? Is he a scene-of-crime policeman bemoaning the fact that he has to attend a murder investigation on a bright day? We could go on suggesting other possibilities for decoding this message, but without further information it would be pure speculation. The words themselves are not difficult to decode but the unpredictability of the last line makes it difficult for us to understand the meaning intended by the speaker.

On the other hand the use of the unexpected and unpredictable in communication may arouse our interest in a way that redundant information does not. It may make us laugh because it is incongruous. Or it may make us stop and think about the message because we cannot immediately decode the meaning. Thus, while the use of entropy can make a message more difficult to decode, it may also increase the possibility that we notice the message and pay more attention to it.

Again this principle is used by advertisers. Instead of producing an advert in which there is a high level of redundancy, with everything easy to decode and predictable, advertisers may opt to include something bizarre, strange, unpredictable – entropic – in order to make us notice the advert and spend time thinking about it.

> **The advert opposite illustrates the principle of entropy. What are the entropic features which make the ad difficult to decode?**
>
> **Compare this ad with the earlier one which contained a high level of redundancy. Which is the more effective and why?**

It may be a matter of personal opinion or preference as to which advert you considered to be the better, but a comparison of the two should show quite clearly the differences between communication which is high in redundancy and that which makes use of the principle of entropy.

> **Imagine you had to produce a slogan for a new brand of soap powder. Using the phrase 'Snow-white Soap Powder is . . .' can you devise six slogans, three of which use the principle of redundancy, and three of which are entropic?**

It is also worth mentioning that it is often the use of entropy in poetry, art, music or literature that makes it interesting and memorable. Like redundancy, entropy is a very useful and practical communication concept.

These useful concepts arose out of consideration of a basically simple, linear model. Shannon and Weaver's model is certainly effective in encouraging further enquiry and debate about communication. But how effective is it in explaining or describing the communication process? For example, the model assumes that communication is an intentional process. And yet we know from our work on NVC that there are often times when communication takes place without a deliberate message being sent. We know, too, that human beings often talk simultaneously, or fail to listen to each other, or send one message with words and a quite different message with gesture or paralinguistics. And, while talking, we are constantly looking for reassurance of feedback that our message is being received, and adjusting our communication to take account of the feedback we get.

These omissions in the Shannon and Weaver model led to criticism that the model was a very imperfect representation of the reality. Subsequent theorists have tried to improve on it.

Feedback

It is relatively easy to convert the linear model (information going direct from sender to destination) into a more circular model, where a number of messages can be sent simultaneously and messages adjusted to take account of feedback, by the simple inclusion of a basic feedback loop into the orginal model. If we added such a loop the model would look like this:

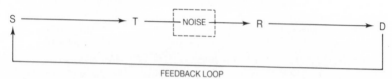

Fig 5.7

An even more complex representation would take into account the fact that there are often a great many additional messages flowing between those involved in face-to-face communication, that some messages are disregarded and never get through to the intended recipient, and that some messages are picked up by those outside the interaction taking place. The model below tries to show something of this complexity.

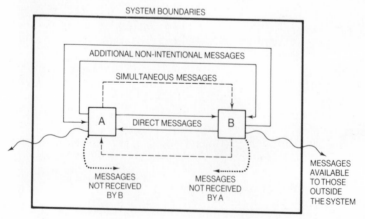

Fig 5.8

The Effects of Attitudes and Individual Perception

Although the model above is a more complex one, there are still many aspects of human communication missing from it – for example, the effects of attitudes and individual perception which, in the Shannon and Weaver model are simply regarded as 'noise'. By the mid-1950s people were beginning to question whether these aspects could be dismissed as noise. Another theorist, Gerbner, felt that they were a fundamental feature of human communication. His theory was that human beings are constantly making choices about which of many pieces of information they will transmit, and about the transmitter, channel and code they will use for transmission. The final choice of what message to send will be determined by how any individual perceives a given event and what he or she considers to be important to communicate about that event.

What we perceive and choose to communicate about an event may also influence our choice of transmission method. A simple observation about the weather may be transmitted immediately via the human voice. An important business decision may be transmitted in a more permanent form via a letter. In both cases the sender of the information will have decided – consciously or subconsciously – how much of what he could say he will say on that occasion.

On the other hand, the choice of channel or transmitter may itself place constraints on the message and increase the number of choices which the sender has to make. In presenting information via a televised news broadcast, for example, the broadcaster has a very limited time to get the information across and will have to be very selective about how much of any news he can transmit. The newspaper journalist may be able to say more, or say it from a more biased perspective, but will also have to make choices about what to include or exclude.

The recipient of information also has to make choices – about whether to receive the information, how much of the information to attend to, and how to interpret the information received. Gerbner therefore produced a model which tried to take account of these individual differences in perception and the process of selection involved in communication. Like Shannon and Weaver, he assumed that the 'correct' meaning of the message would be the one intended by the sender.

The model produced by Gerbner is more complex than that produced by Shannon and Weaver and it encourages us to view communication not simply as a process of transmission but also as one of selection of content.

Gerbner's Model

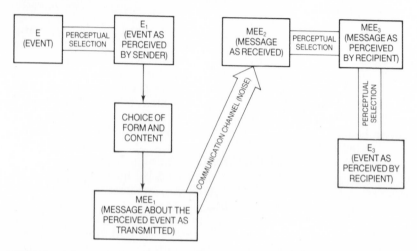

Fig 5.9   Adaptation of Gerbner's Model

Examine Gerbner's model using the key provided. Do you find it helpful in explaining the communication process, or in encouraging you to think about what happens when we communicate? How well would you have understood the model without the verbal explanation given above? What aspects of communication have been omitted from this model?

What you may have discovered is that although the model illustrates the kind of complex choices we have to make in transmitting or receiving information and in the selection of content, it does not address the question of the meaning of the content.

From the 1930s onwards the question of meaning in communication has been studied primarily by philosophers and linguists. They start with a completely different premise from that of Shannon and Weaver. They regard 'meaning', not transmission, as the most important aspect of the communication process. A message may be transmitted and received accurately but the content of the message may not be understood in the same way by the sender and the recipient. One reason for differences in understanding is, of course, the perceptual and attitudinal differences referred to earlier. But there is another reason. The context in which the information is received may affect the meaning the recipient reads into it. And even when there is no deliberate attempt by another person to comunicate with us we may still read meaning into a situation and seek to understand it as if a deliberate act of transmission were taking place.

Unlike Gerbner and Shannon and Weaver, they do not believe that there is a 'correct' meaning for any message. They believe that the meaning of any message is determined by who is interpreting the message at the time. The meaning is not contained in the message but exists only as an interpretation in the mind of the person who is decoding the message.

Semiotics

This group of theorists belongs to what is known as the semiotic school of communication theory. Semiotic theorists accept that messages have to be transmitted, but they are less interested in the process of transmission than in how we interpret and ascribe meaning to messages sent.

Look at this sign. What do you think it represents?

A

What about this one?

B

And this?

C

Fig 5.10

We can't know how you interpreted the first of these signs. One of our students suggested that it was a sheep's back end as the sheep moved away! Nor can we be sure how you interpreted the second. But we suspect that you saw the third one as either a tree or a nuclear explosion. Certainly that is how most of our students saw it. They felt it was a more obvious sign than either of the other two.

Semiotics is the study of signs – a sign being defined as something which stands for something other than itself. The sign acquires a meaning as a result of the use to which it is put, how it is understood by those observing the sign and by association with the object to which it refers. A sign has no intrinsic meaning of its own. It acquires a meaning only as a result of one or more individuals ascribing meaning to it. The first two signs above were taken to have a whole range of meanings by our students, each of whom associated them with different things. The third sign seemed to stand for something which our students recognized from previous experience of having seen signs like it and there was therefore more consensus about what it meant.

> Can you think of any signs which are in daily use to which most people would ascribe the same meaning?
>
> How have these signs acquired a common meaning? How do you know that they mean what you interpret them to mean?
>
> Could you invent a new sign, a symbol, which would stand for 'fire'? How could you teach other people to recognize that the sign stands for 'fire'?

In semiotic theory it is not only pictorial representations or symbols that are regarded as signs. The combination of letters that go to make up words and phrases in our language are also regarded as signs, in that words stand for or represent the object or concept to which they refer. The symbol you invented above stands for fire in the same way that the word 'fire' stands for something which is burning. But the mental picture or concept we have of something burning – fire – will depend on our own associations with fire, how we feel about fire, and the context in which we find the word. The interpretation of fire in the context of the phrase 'a log fire' is likely to be different from that of 'a forest fire'. And an Eskimo's interpretation of 'a forest fire' would, we suspect, differ from that of an American's.

One of the models produced by an American theorist, Peirce, may help us understand this more clearly.

Peirce's Model

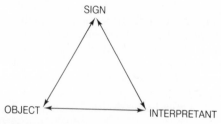

Fig 5.11 Peirce's Model

In this model there is an interactive relationship between the sign, the object to which it refers, and the interpretant who gives meaning to the sign and understands it in a particular way.

The interpretant may be the encoder and sender of a message or the decoder and recipient. The extent to which either interpretant ascribes a similar meaning to the sign will depend on the extent to which they both encounter the sign in the same context and bring to their interpretation similar cultural backgrounds and associations with the object to which the sign refers.

Can you think of any context in which the word 'dog' could be used to mean something other than a four-legged animal? If you can, how did you acquire that knowledge?

We assume that some of our readers have come across alternative meanings for dog – perhaps signifying laziness, or dirtiness, or as a general term of abuse. When and how the word acquired these other meanings we are not sure but, over the years, the fact that the word dog has been associated with these other attributes means that many people can take a similar meaning out of the word when it is used in an uncomplimentary way. Other readers may have had different experiences and have interpreted dog as meaning faithfulness or loyalty or, perhaps, a quite different meaning which we have not thought of.

Over the years different cultures have invented different words to serve the needs of their culture. One linguist, Whorf, pointed out that Eskimos have some 40 or more words to describe snow, whereas in Britain, where snow is less important in our daily lives, we restrict ourselves to about half a dozen words, including 'slush' and 'sleet'. These cultural differences often make it difficult to translate directly from one language to another in such a way that there can be a sharing of meaning. This does not, however, mean that the way one culture interprets a word is any more 'correct' than the way another culture interprets it. Thus Peirce, and others in the semiotic school, would argue that the intended meaning put into a message by the sender is the 'correct' meaning only for the sender. The meaning taken out of it by the recipient is 'correct' for the recipient. If communication is to take place between them there must be enough similarities in their interpretations for them to share a common meaning.

Peirce and other semiotic theorists refer to the agreed meaning of a sign as its *denotative meaning* – we have agreed that this sign will denote this particular object or concept. The individualistic meaning of a sign, which is based on all the connotations and associations the individual has with that sign, is called the *connotative meaning*.

There is a Scottish word 'scunnered' which has no English

equivalent. **The nearest translation is probably 'utterly fed up' but that phrase does not capture the strength of feeling a Scottish speaker might put into the word. Are there any words in the dialect of your local area which people use and understand similarly within that area which do not seem to have a direct translation in standard English? Do you know, or can you find out, why these words have persisted in the local dialect, and why they seem to be useful to retain in that dialect?**

If you can gather together a group of people from different areas of Britain, or with other ethnic origins, it could be interesting to discuss with them how you can begin to arrive at a shared meaning for words which seem to have no direct translation in standard English.

Of course it isn't only words, pictures and symbols that are signs. Objects can also act as signs and stand for something other than themselves. For example, a red flag seen near a quarry during blasting could be interpreted as a denotative sign of danger by those who are aware of the convention of red to signify danger. In a different context, and for those with a particular kind of background and culture, the red flag might be interpreted as a sign of the communist party and the Soviet Union. The same red flag seen on top of a child's sandcastle of the beach might be interpreted as having a completely different meaning – not signifying danger or a political system but as a sign that stands for victory, or exuberance, or simply a child's toy. For some people, remembering their own youth, the flag might evoke feelings of nostalgia and the sign would have a very particular and individualistic connotative meaning ascribed to it by them.

In each case the extent to which we ascribe one of the many possible meanings to the sign will depend on where we see it, and our past associations with the object to which the sign refers. While the flag on the quarry is likely to have been placed there by someone with the deliberate intention to communicate a particular meaning, the flag on top of the sandcastle may not. We cannot know whether the child intended it as an act of communication even though we, as observers of the sign, have read a meaning into it.

The extent to which we cast ourselves in the role of interpretant in relation to any particular sign is also important. We might, for example, have so little interest in a particular sign that we do not consciously ascribe any meaning to it but merely perceive it as being in our environment. When this happens it could be argued that the sign exists without meaning for us as, at that time, we are ascribing no meaning to it.

Try to think up by yourself, or with a partner, further

examples of how signs will depend for their interpretation upon the setting in which they are perceived and the experience of the interpretant.

We said above that there was no single 'correct' interpretation of any message. But, of course, for much of our daily life it is important that the interpretation intended by the sender is shared, at least partially, by that of the recipient. Indeed, if we did not have this kind of sharing, communication of any kind would be impossible and you would be unable to read any of our intended meaning into this book! If someone places a red flag as a sign of danger, it is important for survival that those seeing it interpret the sign as danger and react appropriately.

It is just possible, however, that some people might interpret the sign as danger, but take a deeper meaning out of it and regard the word 'danger' as a sign which they interpret as 'challenge'. In which case, appropriate behaviour for these individuals might be to rise to the challenge and see if they can enter the danger area and escape without injury! In this situation we have a sharing of denotative meaning at one level. The intention that the flag should signify danger has been transmitted to the receiver. But, at a deeper level there is no sharing in the intended meaning since the concept referred to – in this case 'danger' – is itself taken as a sign and interpreted differently by the receiver.

As you can see, we have moved a long way from the assumption that if we transmit the signal effectively the intentions of the sender will be realized! And yet both transmission and meaning are important elements in the communication process. The Shannon and Weaver model and the Peirce model – both very simple models in themselves – provide us with a way of examining these two different approaches and making comparisons between them. The Gerbner model provides a link between the two and gives some indication of the kind of complexity which might be required if we wished to produce a model which would encompass all the different strands that come together in a single act of human communication.

We have examined a very few models of communication and have included some lengthy explanations of these. To what extent could you have understood the concepts from the models alone? To what extent did the models help to clarify the words? How useful are the models we have given as a means of:

explaining aspects of the communication process;
describing aspects of the communication process;
formulating theories about communication;
predicting what will happen in reality;

stimulating discussion and encouraging experimentation in practice?

The Practical Benefits of Models

We would be surprised if you had found the small selection of models we have given here useful in all of the areas above. As authors, we have used the models to provide a framework which allowed us to discuss the different aspects of the communication procress in isolation. Now that you know what the models mean, they provide a shorthand method for referring to different theories. The TR model probably now has more meaning for you than it had at the start of the chapter. In later chapters, when we talk about transmission we can simply refer to the model, rather than having to repeat the theoretical considerations behind it.

The very act of trying to model communication helps us realize just how complex it is. Before Shannon and Weaver produced their model there was a fairly general assumption that communication was a simple process. As a result of their work, and the work of others in the field, it soon became apparent that effective transmission of information was far more complex than anyone had realized. The practical result of such theorizing is that there is now a whole industry devoted to finding new, more efficient and faster methods of transmitting large quantities of information over vast distances; and we already have access to communication technology far more powerful than our grandparents could have imagined.

Similarly, the work of Peirce and others has led to a study of how we interpret signs and has helped us to develop signs and symbols which are universally acceptable and to which we all agree to ascribe the same denotative meaning. For example, people throughout the world have now agreed to use the same symbol for radio-activity. This has an obvious practical benefit if we wish to avoid areas of contamination.

Advertising also relies on our ability to interpret the meaning of signs and signals. And consumer products, from soap-powder to furniture rely on pictorial signs to convey such meanings as washing instructions, inflammability or the chemical constituents of the product.

As we try to model communication we find ourselves asking questions. Is this really what happens? Can we predict what might happen if . . .? How can we test our model to see if it works in practice? The very act of asking questions can often lead to exploration of new areas and the opening up of new information that we did not know existed.

In this chapter we have looked at only three constrasting models of human communication. We could go on to look at many more but we do not have the space to do so in this book.

In the meantime we leave you with a challenge:

Can you devise a model that will explain and describe a significant part of human communication? Can you use this model to devise an experiment that will allow you to test the effectiveness of your model? Does it work in practice?

Even if you do not succeed in producing an effective model, we suspect that you will have learned quite a bit about communication from having attempted to produce one.

REFERENCES

ALLEN, K. (1986): *Linguistic meaning* Vols 1 and 2. Routledge & Kegan Paul

BARTHES, R. (1980): *Elements of semiology.* Hill & Wong

COUPLAND, N. (1988): *Styles of discourse.* Routledge

CULLER, J. (1981): *The pursuit of signs.* Routledge

DAVIS, H. & WALTON, P. (1983): *Language, image, media.* Basil Blackwell

GERBNER, G. (1956): Towards a general model of communication. *Audiovisual communication review* 4 (3), 171–91

GOLDING, P. & ELLIOTT, P. (1980): *Making the news.* Longman

GOLDING, P. & MIDDLETON, S. (1982): *Images of welfare.* Martin Robertson

HALLIDAY, M.A.C. (1979): *Language as social semiotic.* Edward Arnold

JAKOBSON, R. (1968): *Child language: aphasia and general sound laws.* Mouton

PEARSON, J.C. (1985): *Gender and communication.* Wm C. Brown

PEIRCE, C.S. (1931–58): *Collected papers.* Harvard University Press

SEBEOK, T. (ed.) (1977): *A perfusion of signs.* Indiana University Press

SHANNON, C. & WEAVER, W. (1949): *The mathematical theory of communication.* University of Illinois Press

SLESS, D. (1986): *In search of semiotics.* Routledge

WHORF, B.L. (1956): *Language, thought and reality.* Wiley

CHAPTER SIX
ROLES AND RELATIONSHIPS

All the world's a stage,
And all the men and women merely players;
They have their exits and their entrances,
And one man in his time plays many parts . . .

When Shakespeare wrote these words he wasn't suggesting that we all go through life pretending to be something we're not – playing at life, rather than living. He was simply pointing out what most of realize instinctively to be true – the fact that all of us, in a single day, display many different kinds of behaviour depending on the situations we find outselves in.

Luigi Pirandello, a twentieth-century Italian dramatist, also took this as his theme in a play called *Six Characters in Search of an Author*. One of the characters in the play has this to say:

> My drama lies entirely in this one thing. . . . In my being conscious that each one of us believes himself to be a single person. But it's not true. . . . Each one of us is many persons . . . according to all the possibilities of being that are within us. With some people we are one person. With others we are somebody quite different. And all the time we are under the illusion of always being one and the same person for everybody. We believe we are always this one person in whatever it is we may be doing.

In this extract Pirandello is expressing something else which we all instinctively believe in – the concept of self-identity and the feeling we have in ourselves of being a unique individual with a personality which is recognizably our own.

The semiotic perspective on communication, which we dealt with in the previous chapter, takes the uniqueness of the individual as a premise for the view that individual differences make it impossible for human beings to take exactly the same meaning out of any sign or message. Thus communication is seen as a process of negotiation in which each person involved in sending or receiving a message seeks for some common ground on which they can agree. Shared experience, a common culture, common usage of linguistic signs and contextual cues all help in the search for an agreed meaning which serves as a vehicle for exchanging ideas and forming relationships.

Yet it is in our different relationships with other people that the most obvious differences in our role behaviours occur. So how can we reconcile this feeling of being a single, unified and unique personality, with the fact that we display a whole range of different and even conflicting behaviours in our communication and relationships with others? Is there a bit of us which exists independently of all the roles we play, and which could be called the 'self'? Or is our 'self', or personality, simply the sum total of all the roles we hold, and the behaviour we display in these roles?

In this chapter we try to find an answer to some of these questions. We clarify what is meant by roles and role behaviour. We look at role conflict and the concept of self, and we examine some of the ways in which our role behaviour affects our relationships and the ways in which we communicate with others in a variety of different situations.

Roles and Role Behaviour

Sociologists and psychologists make a distinction between the roles we hold and the behaviour we display in carrying out these roles (Goffman, 1961; Berger, 1966; Argyle, 1983; Ornstein; 1987).

> *Roles are the positions we hold in life relative to other people. They indicate our status and the relationship we have to others, but do not tell us how a particular individual will behave in any given role.*
> *Role behaviour, or role enactment, is the term used to refer to the way in which an individual carries out a particular role.*

For example, in relation to my parents I hold the role of child. Yet, in relation to my child I hold the role of mother. I am an aunt to my nieces and nephews, a lecturer to students, a patient to my doctor, a wife to my husband – and so on. Each of these different roles makes different demands on me. Each calls forth different behaviours, and these behaviours are largely dependent on how I perceive my role in each situation. Knowing that I hold these roles gives you some general information about my status and relationships, but in order to learn about me as an individual you would require to observe my behaviour when carrying out particular roles.

Very quickly jot down all the roles you can think of that you hold in life. Beside each one note down one or two keywords that might characterize your behaviour in that role.

Note how many times you have used the same keywords – suggesting that your role behaviours in these roles may be similar – and whether there are any roles in which the keyword is so completely different that it stands out.

> Can you explain the similarities and differences in your role behaviour?
>
> Are there any roles in which you feel you are 'more yourself' than others. Can you explain why?
>
> If you are working with others perhaps you could take a few minutes to discuss these points.

As with so many of the exercises in this book, we have no way of knowing how our readers answered the questions; but we would be very surprised if anyone had used exactly the same keywords to characterize every role. We suspect that the majority of readers used a range of keywords of varying degrees of similarity, and that the keywords which differed most related to those roles in which the person felt a need to conform to certain norms of behaviour.

In some jobs, for example, there are rules of behaviour – either written or understood – with which the employee is expected to comply even though the behaviours required may be very different from those the person displays when not at work. Similarly, in certain social situations – such as a wedding, a funeral, going to church or attending a football match, for example – most people display the kinds of behaviour that they perceive to be appropriate and socially acceptable in that situation.

We are also fairly confident that the majority of readers included in their lists of roles some that were *assigned*, some which were *chosen*, some which might be called *referential* and others which were more *casual*.

Assigned Roles

Assigned roles are ones which have been determined for us by other people, by birth or as a result of other factors over which we have no control. Sex roles would come into this category, as would our role as child and all the other roles assigned to us as a result of our birth position within a family – sister, brother, aunt, cousin, etc. Apart from a campaign of mass murder we have virtually no way of avoiding holding these roles! What we can control is how we carry them out. How we choose to behave as, for example, a grandchild, will depend partly on our feelings for our grandparents, and partly on what we have learned is appropriate behaviour in that relationship. Thus two people, each holding the role of grandchild, might display very different behaviours in that role. Similarly, one brother might feel it a necessary part of his role to spend time caring for a younger member of the family. Another might not see that as part of his role at all. And, of course, though everyone has a role as either a male or a female, how each of us defines that role and carries it out will depend on the whole range of genetic and learned factors that we discussed in Chapters One and Two.

Without looking back at Chapter Two, can you recall the ways in which attitudes about appropriate behaviour are formed? If you cannot, it would perhaps be a good idea to read over that chapter before proceeding here. If you can, try answering these questions:

In your role as male or female, to what extent does your role behaviour conform to what you perceive to be the traditional role of a man or woman? Why?

Are there occasions when you behave in a stereotyped male or female role? If not, why not? If so, what causes this behaviour?

Are there occasions when you wish someone else would behave in a more conventional, or stereotyped sex-role? If so, why? And how does their behaviour affect your role behaviour?

Are there any differences in the way you communicate when you are with people of the same sex and with people of the opposite sex? If not, why not? If so, why, and how to these changes in communication affect your role as a male or female?

We suspect that most of our readers do exhibit some changes, in communicating with members of the same or opposite sex – even if these changes are fairly small and subtle. One reason is the different way we identify with and relate to people of either sex. In some of these relationships we will have ideas about how the other person expects us to behave and we may try to live up to these expectations. Or the way they relate to us in our role as male or female may affect the particular types of behaviour we are prepared to engage in.

Another reason is that although we retain the same sex-role in each situation, we have added an additional role to it. We have, at the simplest level, changed our role from simply that of man or woman to that of male or female communicator. In doing so we have added to our repertoire of role behaviour those aspects which we regard as appropriate to communication in that situation. Depending on who the other people are, we may also have added other roles such as friend, acquaintance, partner, fellow-student, etc. Their expectations of our role behaviour may also subtly affect not only what we choose to talk about but the general mannerisms and language we use in doing so.

In some situations the roles of partner, friend, acquaintance, etc., may also be assigned to us, whether we want to hold these roles or not. For example, someone may have assigned to us the role of friend, even though we ourselves would regard our role as merely acquaintance. We may behave in ways which we would regard as being inappropriate in a friend but still, in the eyes of the other person, we have been designated the role of friend and will be regarded as a friend unless or until we can convince the other person that the role we have been assigned is not an appropriate one. A similar situation may occur at work when someone assigns us the role of 'general dogsbody' even though that is not how we see our role! In this case it may be very difficult to convince the other that the role assigned to us is an inappropriate one, and certainly not the one we assumed we were choosing when we took the job.

> **Look back at the list of roles you made earlier. Can you identify the assigned roles on that list? Are there any assigned roles which you have omitted and you feel you ought to have included? If there are, how important are these roles to you?**

Sometimes we hold assigned roles which simply act as labels. These labels indicate that we hold the roles, but the roles themselves are not important to us and we may not engage in any specific behaviour associated with that role. We may, for example, hold the role of cousin but the role is not one that is important to us because we never make contact with that cousin and do not have any personal interactions with the person concerned.

Sometimes, too, we are 'stuck' with an assigned role that we have to perform, even though we don't particularly want to do so. An example of this would be the role of child, or elderly person. Even though the child tries to behave in the most adult way imaginable, the assigned role of child is with him until he grows up. The elderly person might long to be young again, and might engage in behaviour similar to that of youth but we can't put the clock back and the assigned role remains whether we like it or not.

In many cases, however, the role assigned to us by other people is congruent with the role we would choose in relation to them. We may be happy to be grandparents, with all the connotations of age that go with the role. Friendship roles may be reciprocated. If someone has assigned us the role of partner we may be willing to accept the role. Or we know we are regarded as office juniors and expect others to relate to us in that role – which may include being treated as a 'general dogsbody'!

Chosen Roles

Unlike assigned roles which are determined by situations which are largely outwith our control, chosen roles are ones which we have determined for ourselves. These would include occupational roles (the jobs we have chosen to work at); social roles (the clubs of which we are members or the roles we hold in our spare time); friendship roles; and roles like wife, husband, parent, etc. Again, once we have opted for a particular role, the way in which we carry it out will depend on a whole range of factors, many of which will be similar to those which operate in our assigned roles.

> **Can you identify the chosen roles on your list? For how many of these chosen roles did you feel you were able to make a completely free choice, without being constrained by factors outside your control? How many of these chosen roles do you now feel you can abandon without causing concern to yourself or others. If you were completely free to redesign your life, how many of your existing assigned or chosen roles would you choose to adopt? And what other choices would you make if there were no constraints on your choice?**

We suspect that most people found that their chosen roles were, to some extent, constrained by factors not entirely within their control. Friendship choices, for example, may be determined by who we come into contact with. Similarly, the occupational role may be determined not only by qualifications, aptitudes and experience, but also by the jobs that are available and the extent to which we feel free to travel in order to take up work.

Referential Roles

The constraints we experience in choosing particular roles may be governed by very real and pressing circumstances. Poverty, illness, inability to move because of family commitments etc., may be aspects of our life over which we have relatively little control and we may have to take these factors into account both when choosing a role and in the performance of that role. There are, however, other constraints which are more psychological. These arise out of our perception of what is appropriate role behaviour, and they may be determined by the referential roles we hold in life.

Referential roles may be either assigned or chosen. In either case they imply a general role which is dependent on our being members of a group which has specific and identifiable characteristics. 'Wife', for example, is a role which denotes that someone has something in common with all other wives – in this case marital status. But in any culture the term 'wife' will be commonly accepted to have other attributes that apply to the role of wife and act as a reference point for how one is expected to perform the role within that culture. Even if someone elects to perform the role in a different manner, knowledge of what is expected still provides a reference point for departure from the accepted norm.

'John's wife', on the other hand, is not referential. It is specific to one person in a particular relationship. There is no general class of people who have recognizable characteristics as a 'John's wife'! And there are no culturally determined expectations about how John's wife should behave in her particular role.

Nevertheless, even though 'John's wife' is a unique role the general referential expectations of wifely behaviour may very well affect her in carrying out her role. Similarly John will have expectations about how he is expected to behave in the referential role of husband. He will also have referential expectations of appropriate behaviour in a wife. If there is a high degree of congruence in the way John and his wife interpret these referential roles, there may be little conflict between them as to what is appropriate role behaviour for each.

If, however, two people in a relationship have markedly different expectations about their own or the other person's referential role behaviour, this can lead to disagreements and, in severe situations, to a total breakdown in the relationship. Either or both partners may seek to change the other's role behaviour to bring it more into line with what is expected. One partner may be dominant, forcing the other to adopt the expected behaviour; or manipulative, attempting to achieve the same result by more devious means. Or one member may simply adapt voluntarily. In this case there may be fewer overt conflicts in the relationship but the individual who has adapted may feel internal conflict like that experienced in cognitive dissonance because there may be a discrepancy between role behaviour engaged in and personal attitudes about how the role ought to be performed.

Readers who have familiarized themselves with Chapter Two will no doubt have noticed that referential roles bear more than a passing resemblance to stereotypes. Both are based on specific characteristics which are easily identified in a group. Both imply associated characteristics which are attributed to members of that group and create expectations about what group members will say and do. The difference is that stereotypes represent a quick classification system that can be *applied to describe members of a group*, whereas referential roles are *held by those who are members of the group*. Stereotypes about the way members of the group should behave become role models which the individuals can use as a reference for role behaviour as a member of the group.

Role Conflict

There can be occasions when we are so conscious of the referential expectations associated with a role that we believe we have to exhibit the expected behaviour even when it does not feel natural to behave in that way. We may conform outwardly but feel that what we are doing or saying is not right for us. Or we may want to carry out referential roles according to what is expected but be physically or emotionally incapable of doing so. In these situations there can be considerable psychological distress because the person is conscious of performing a role in a way that is not compatible with their own concept of themselves. This can give rise to feelings of guilt at being hypocritical, and fear that the hypocrisy might be found out. We may feel inadequate because we can't feel or do everything that is expected of us, angry and frustrated that we have been assigned roles we don't want to perform, or envious of others who seem able to perform their roles with ease.

These feelings stem from role conflict – literally a conflict between what we do and what we believe we ought to do or want to do in performing a given role. Psychoanalysts and social workers who work with severly depressed or emotionally disturbed patients have argued that many of the so-called personality disorders like schizophrenia, neuroticism, phobias and obsessions may be traceable back to their origins in role conflict either at the present time or in an earlier stage of life (Laing, 1959; Smail, 1984). If individuals can be encouraged to change their role expectations or to accept that their own behaviour is not so out of phase with the norm they may begin to show some improvement in the symptoms they display.

Another form of conflict is that experienced when the different roles held by an individual, and normally performed separately from each other, come together or overlap in some way. One of our mature students explained how she came to experience role conflict of this kind. During the day she performed the role of student, but when she went home in the evening she reverted to the role of mother, inter-acting with her children until they were in bed and asleep, when she once more adopted the role of student, reading textbooks or writing up assignments. With the roles kept separate in this way she was able to perform both to her own satisfaction. But on one particular evening she felt a strong pressure to adopt the role of student (an important essay was due to be finished and handed in the next day!) but kept being interrupted to act as a caring mother to one of her children who had developed a minor illness. She described her feeling of guilt at not performing the mother's role as wholeheartedly as she should. At the same time she felt anger and frustration that her role as student was being disrupted.

Working wives and mothers, because of the sheer number of roles they hold, not infrequently experience this type of role conflict. Men also experience conflicts when the demands of their jobs seem to be at odds with the demands of their roles as husband or father. And within the work place itself many people experience role conflict when they feel they want to perform their job in a particular way, that they ought to perform it in that way, but that they are unable to do so because of the many conflicting demands made on them by their various roles in relation to other people within the organization.

The theme of role conflict – either between people, or within an individual – is one which many novelists and dramatists have used in their work.

Can you identify any novels you have read or plays you have seen recently in which the story line was clearly based on role conflicts? How did the characters cope with or resolve the conflict? How true to life did the conflicts appear? And how, if you had been one of the characters, would you have performed the roles differently?

Fictional accounts can provide remarkably accurate insights into role conflict and its resolution. Reading such accounts can sometimes suggest ways out of our own dilemmas. They may highlight the fact that our own conflict is not unusual and this may make it easier for us to talk about it. Just as talking with a psychoanalyst or social worker may help the severely emotionally disturbed person, so a good 'moaning session' with friends, or other people experiencing similar role conflicts, can often reduce the psychological unease we feel.

Another way of dealing with role conflict is to cast ourselves in the role of author and to write our own fictional account – perhaps in the form of a short story – of a character experiencing role conflict similar to our own. As we take control in the story of the character's life and try to predict the effects of the conflict on him or her, we may not only gain insights into our own problems, but also learn to take control of our own lives in such a way that we can exercise some choices which will help reduce the role conflict we are experiencing.

Try writing either a couple of pages, or a complete short story on the theme of role conflict. Even if you do not consider it to be very good, it should be interesting to compare and discuss what you have written with what other people have written on the same topic. If it it good, who knows? . . . you might have the start of a full-length novel!

Casual Roles

There is one final type of role which we need to mention – the casual role. Assigned and chosen roles tend to be recognized as roles by the individual concerned, and to be of relatively long duration or have some importance in the person's life. Casual roles last only a few moments, a few hours, or a few days. We slip in and out of them easily and we do not make a great psychological investment in performing the role. Casual roles are ones which simply occur as a result of our being in a particular situation. When journeying by train we hold the role of traveller; when eating, diner; and when in the high street, pedestrian or driver, shopper or consumer.

Strangely enough, although we slip into many of these casual roles easily and automatically, the roles themselves are often ones which are associated with very specific codes of acceptable role behaviour.

In Britain, for example, it is appropriate for bus travellers to join a queue and to file into the bus in orderly fashion. In shops and self-service supermarkets it is not generally expected that people will prod or taste the produce before buying. But in some European countries getting on a bus is a 'free-for-all' in which people accept that pushing and jostling is a normal part of the process. Similarly, in European food markets it is often considered the mark of an inept shopper not to prod or taste the goods in order to establish their quality.

Self-Image and the Concept of Self

Paradoxically, it is when engaged in performing the learned behaviours associated with the performance of these casual roles, that we often feel most 'ourselves'. The psychologist Robert Ornstein explains this by suggesting that many of these casual roles are performed alone, or in relatively minimal or non-intimate contact with others. The learned role behaviours can be performed under only a small portion of our mind's control, leaving the rest of our mind free to plan, to dream, to worry or to think about whatever we choose (Ornstein, 1987).

When we are engaged in this kind of mental activity it is as if we were communicating with ourselves, performing, as it were, in the role of self for the benefit of ourselves as audience. This mental communication, because it does not involve anyone else, seems to provide us with empirical proof that we exist as individuals who have a 'secret self' that need not be made manifest to other people in our role dealings with them. And it is perhaps significant that most people would use the phrase 'being myself' to refer to situations when they are either alone and not required to 'perform' for the benefit of other people, or in situations where no one seems to be making demands that require them to make an effort to respond in an appropriate way.

It is also revealing that many people use the sentence 'I can relax and be myself' when talking about their behaviour within their own home – either alone or with people who know them well and with whom they are prepared to share some of their innermost thoughts and feelings. We have already noted that role conflict creates psychological tension. If we have a feeling that we can relax when 'being ourselves', perhaps it is because we are either not performing according to any role expectations or, alternatively, we are engaging only in those role behaviours which we ourselves have determined using our own secret ideas, feelings and thoughts as our reference for what is acceptable.

Within the English language there are a great many phrases used to indicate this discrepancy between role behaviour which is determined by external reference groups, or by the expectations of others, and behaviour which is determined primarily by what 'feels' right, natural or comfortable for the person concerned. Sentences like 'It just wasn't me', or 'I couldn't be myself with him' reveal our deeply rooted sense of self.

> **How many common English phrases and sentences can you find that refer to being or not being ourselves? If you know someone from a culture in which a language different from English is spoken, discuss with them whether they have phrases in their language which show this sense of self. Perhaps they have a different denotative meaning for the term self and can offer an explanation of what it means to them? Even discussion with someone from your own culture may well reveal interesting differences in what you mean when you say you are 'being yourself'.**

Another reason which helps explain our consciousness of self is the awareness of our own body as an entity separate from the bodies of others. However much our behaviour changes in the course of a day, we are aware that it is the same physical body that performs these different behaviours. We may make different gestures in different situations but it is the same hands that we use for all. We use the same vocal cords to produce a whole range of different types of language and accent, the same face to express different emotions and the same brain to process the myriad of items of information coming at us from a whole range of different sources. Consciousness of the constancy of our body gives us a sense of personal, stable and continuing identity. When we feel pain or anger we are conscious that it is our own body, our self, which is experiencing these feelings. We may express our emotions differently in different situations but we are aware that the feelings remain recognizably our own.

The physical evidence of our body and emotions, coupled with the knowledge that we can engage in mental activity, an inner life which we are not required to reveal to anyone else, provides a fairly adequate explanation of why we have a sense of self-identity. What it does not explain is the other concept of self-image – literally an image of our personality that we hold constant even when we are conscious that we are behaving 'out of character'.

In Chapter Two when we talked about people behaving out of character we suggested that we either did not know them well enough to predict accurately how they would behave, or that they were exhibiting behaviours which seemed to reveal an aspect of themselves out of keeping with what we had come to expect from them. Yet when we talk about ourselves as behaving out of character we seem to be suggesting that we know ourselves so well that we are aware that our behaviour is not a natural part of what we regard as our personality, and that we have deliberately chosen on this occasion to behave like someone other than ourselves.

The Swiss psychologist Piaget offers one explanation of how we develop a self-image and a consciousness of our own personality. He argues that very young children have no sense of themselves as separate beings. When they inadvertently bang their heads with their fist they are not conscious that they are themselves the cause of the pain they feel. They are not yet mature enough to distinguish between self and other, or self and object. They do not realize that physical objects remain even when they cannot be perceived by the senses, and they have no sense of causality – they do not know what causes things to happen, simply that they do happen. Gradually, as a result of maturation and interaction with their environment, they develop these concepts and become aware of the difference between self, other people and inanimate objects.

Later, with the development of language, they begin to form concepts of 'who' this separate being is. They learn from what is said about them by others that this self of theirs is 'a good boy' or 'a big boy' or 'Mary's little brother'. They begin to associate certain feelings and actions with these labels. All of this information is gradually absorbed to produce a sense of self which is a composite of all that they have learned about themselves in interactions with others and with their physical environment.

For example, a child may find himself experiencing an emotion which he recognizes as fear when asked by his parents to jump into a swimming pool. If he loves and trusts his parents he may do as asked and be rewarded by being told how brave and clever he is. If a child has a repeated number of such experiences he is likely to grow up having an image of himself as a brave and clever person – one who may feel fear like everyone else, but whose personality is such that he can conquer the fear and 'take the plunge'. In later life we might well recognize him as the entrepreneur who is not afraid to take risks in his business and is willing try out new courses of action.

On the other hand, a child who receives a great many contradictory signals about who he is – for example, brave and clever one minute but stupid and a nuisance the next – will find it difficult to establish a coherent self-image and may either spend much of his later life in attempting to work out what his own personality is, or he may learn to ignore what others say about him and gradually build up an image of himself based on what he does and says in different situations and how he feels when doing so. Those words and actions which bring satisfaction or rewards – which feel good – may very well be the basis on which he builds his self-image.

This is only one explanation of how self-image and the concept of personality is formed. There are many others. Eysenck suggests that it is genetic endowment which leads to naturally passive, aggressive, extroverted, introverted, anxious or obsessive personalities (Eysenck, 1967). Other theorists have tried to show that there are a number of recognizable clusters of character traits which almost always go together and allow us to distinguish different personality types (Cattell, 1965; Allport, 1961). Freud (1946) believed it was the extent of a person's inherited sexual drive which was the main determinant of personality. While behaviourists such as Skinner (1957) and Bandura (1963) argue that each individual's personality is shaped by learning and imitation of others.

Encounter and T-Groups

Regardless of which theory is the correct one, it is undoubtedly true that adults who lack a clear self-image often feel unhappy and emotionally disturbed. They may seek help in groups such as encounter groups or sensitivity training groups known as T-groups (Moreno, 1945; Rogers, 1965; Douglas, 1976). These groups meet together under the guidance of a trained psychologist who helps the individuals in the group to understand what is happening in their encounters with others and to become more sensitive in recognizing their own and other people's feelings and needs. Groups like these provide opportunities to express how one sees oneself in the company of others who will give their honest opinion of how far the perceived self seems to be obvious in behaviour. Using techniques based on role-play, word association, trying to imagine what one would be if translated into an appropriate object or animal, or exercise involving analysis of movement, speech and gesture, these groups may enable a person gradually to build up a consistent and acceptable self-image and, in the process, can help transform an emotionally disturbed person into one who is more emotionally stable and capable of taking control of his or her life.

Some firms, particularly in America, offer their employees the chance to participate in groups of this kind. In this situation the aim is not so much to establish self-image and reduce emotional instability. Rather, there is a recognition of the kind of role conflicts that often exist between and within individuals in an organization. These groups aim to help people explore and resolve role conflicts, and reduce occupational stress and tensions. The idea behind this is that the work force will become more contented and cohesive and will work together more effectively, with the result that the efficiency and productivity of the firm will improve.

Transactional Analysis

There is another technique which is used quite a lot in helping people understand and resolve role conflicts. This technique, developed by a pscychologist named Eric Berne, is called Transactional Analysis (TA). Berne's theories are based on the premise that human beings, in their early years, derive both sustenance and comfort from the physical contact they have with their parents. The cuddles and loving words given to them as children (what Berne calls positive strokes) are taken as a sign that they are loved and therefore worthy of love. Smacks or harsh words (negative strokes) may send out the opposite message. The child may try to adapt behaviour in order to become more worthy and receive more positive stroking. Gradually the child builds up an image of self as a worthy or unworthy person depending on the amount of positive stroking received from parents, or other adults who are regarded as significant.

A child who does not receive enough physical or verbal stroking may grow up without any clear sense of self-worth. The lack of stroking may be felt as a greater pschological deprivation than negative strokes as it implies that the child does not matter as a person. Her existence is not recognized – either physically or verbally – by those adults on whom she depends.

When a child becomes an adult she may have a need to reaffirm her own self-image as a worthy or unworthy person by seeking to obtain strokes from other people. In adulthood these strokes may be physical – a hug, a push, etc. – but the most common strokes will be verbal, occurring in conversation with others. When the boss says 'that was a good piece of work you did last week' this represents a positive stroke. 'What kind of work do you call this? It's terrible' is obviously negative. A smile, and a murmured hello when we meet someone we know is a positive stroke. A frown, or a lack of the expected greeting, may be taken as a negative stroke or as a lack of stroking.

In childhood we also learn how to give other people strokes which are either negative or positive so that they will reciprocate by giving us the kind of stroking we want. Our preference might be for positive strokes, but negative strokes are better than nothing. If giving a parent a hug and saying 'I love you' does not evoke a response, pouring ink over the lounge carpet may ensure that negative strokes follow! In time, we learn to recognize those people likely to respond to us with either positive or negative strokes and to behave in the way likely to call forth from them the stroking we need.

Most of the time, of course, we are not conscious of deliberately trying to evoke a particular kind of stroking behaviour. The motivation seems to stem from a deeper, more unconscious level of the mind. But the theory goes some way towards explaining some of our more enduring personality traits – such as wanting to please, being afraid to say no, trying to keep the peace and avoid rows at all costs, deliberate aggression or a need to show off and demonstrate how clever we are.

It also helps explain why we behave differently in different role relationships. Making flattering remarks to one person might be a good way of getting them to regard us favourably and reward us with positive strokes. With other people such tactics might have the opposite effect, or no effect at all. One boss may be very appreciative of punctuality, another may be a stickler for detail, or for ensuring that staff present the right image. Adaptions in behaviour towards others may be most marked in relation to those we regard as significant – either because we care about them and their opinion of us matters, or because they have status and power over us.

People with a strong positive self-image may feel less need for stroking and show less marked changes in role behaviour. Maslow (1987) has described such people as self-actualizing. They feel confident enough to do without stroking, to set their own course of action and to take responsibility for their own lives.

We will be looking at other aspects of Berne's and Maslow's theories in the next two chapters, where we examine roles and relationships in the context of group and organizational communication.

Summary

1 Each human being holds many different roles.

2 Roles may be assigned, chosen, referential or casual.

3 Role refers to a position in life relative to other people. Role behaviour or role-enactment refers to how roles are performed.

4 Referential roles are based on stereotyped expectations of acceptable role behaviour; some people strive to meet these expectations with, or without success; others deliberately avoid doing so.

5 Role-conflict occurs when role expectations cannot be met, when expectations between people differ, or when roles are incompatible.

6 Human beings believe they have a self which is separate from their roles: various explanations of how self-image is acquired have been put forward.

7 People who lack a sense of self or self-worth may find help in groups specifically designed to increase self awareness.

8 Transactional Analysis provides some explanations for differences in role behaviour.

9 How we communicate in any given role will be determined by role-expectations – our own and those of others – personality, conformity, need for stroking and self-actualization.

REFERENCES

ALLPORT, G. (1961): *Patterns and growth in personality*. Penguin

ARGYLE, M. (1983): *The social psychology of work*. Pelican

BANDURA, A. & WALTERS, R.H. (1963): *Social learning and personality development*. Holt, Rinehart & Winston

BERGER, P. (1966): *Invitation to sociology*. Penguin

BERNE, E. (1961): *TA in psychotherapy*. Souvenir press

CATTELL, R.B. (1965): *The scientific analysis of personality.* Penguin.

DOUGLAS, R. (1976): *Groupwork practice.* Tavistock

EYSENCK, H. (1967): *The biological basis of personality.* Thomas Springfield

FREUD, A. (1964): *The ego and the mechanisms of defence.* International Universities Press

GOFFMAN, E. (1961): *Asylums.* Anchor Books

LAING, R.D. (1959): *The divided self.* Penguin

MASLOW, A.H. (1987): *Motivation and personality.* Harper & Row

MORENO, J.L. (1945): *Psychodrama.* Beacon House

ORNSTEIN, R.E. (1987): *The psychology of consciousness*; Harcourt Brace Jovanovich

PIAGET, J. & INHILDER, B. (1958): *The growth of logical thinking*; Routledge & Kegal Paul

PIRANDELLO, L. (1954): *Six characters in search of an author.* Heinemann

PULASKI, M.A.S. (1980): *Understanding Piaget.* Harper & Row

ROGERS, C.R. (1965): *On becoming a person.* Houghton-Mifflin

SKINNER, B.F. (1957): *Verbal behaviour.* Appleton-Century Crofts

SMAIL, D. (1984): *Illusion and reality.* Dent

FURTHER READING

BARKER, D. (1980): *TA and training.* Gower

BARNES, P. (1984): *Personality, development and learning.* Open University text. Hodder & Stoughton

BURNS, R.B. (1979): *The self-concept.* Longman

COOK, M. (1982): *Perceiving others.* Methuen

EISNER, J.S. (1986): *Social psychology.* Cambridge University Press

ERIKSEN, E. (1972): *Childhood and security.* Pelican

GRAHAM, H. (1986): *The human face of psychology.* Oxford University Press

NELSON-JONES, R. (1986): *Human relationship skills.* Holt, Rinehart & Winston

STEWART, I. & JOINES, V.A. (1987): *TA today – a new introduction to TA.* Lifespace Publishing

ZURCHER, L.A. (1983): *Social roles: conformity, conflict and creativity.* Sage

CHAPTER SEVEN
COMMUNICATION IN GROUPS

Take five minutes to jot down a list of all the groups of which you are a member. How would you define 'group' and 'group membership'?

It would not be surprising if readers found some difficulty in arriving at a definition which covered all the types of groups of which they were members. A definition which suited the small, intimate group (often called a Primary Group) is unlikely to serve so well to describe a larger, more impersonal grouping (the Secondary Group), or a referential group of the type discussed in the previous chapter.

Membership of the Primary Group will involve regular contact and direct face-to-face communication with other members in the group. Membership of a Secondary Group may require much less direct contact and personal involvement, while membership of a referential group could imply anything from strong identification with the norms of that group to simple awareness that one shares characteristics in common with other members.

We have already explored many aspects of the referential group, and in the next chapter we turn our attention to communication within larger groups and organizations. For the purposes of this chapter, therefore, we will concentrate on the characteristics of the small Primary Group, the roles adopted within such a group and the communication processes involved.

What Characterizes the Primary Group?

In 1909 an American sociologist, Charles Cooley, coined the term 'Primary' as a means of defining a small group (2–20 people) who regularly associate and co-operate with each other and who share some common purpose. Other sociologists have added to this definition. Thomas (1967) suggested that members of a Primary Group are not only aware of their membership but are aware of the boundaries of the group – i.e. they know what distinguishes their group from another and they know who all the members of their group are. Hare (1962) argues that the knowledge of 'who members of the group are' leads to a complicated set of unwritten (and sometimes written) rules which govern role-behaviour and interaction. Cartwright & Zander (1953) coined the term 'Group Dynamics' to describe the changing patterns and flows of interaction and communication which occur.

Using the criteria suggested above, can you identify, from the list you made earlier, the Primary Groups of which you are a member?

What Purpose Does a Primary Group Serve?

A number of writers have suggested that it is useful, in looking at the purpose of a group, to distinguish between the 'naturally occurring' small group and the 'created group' (Argyle, 1983; Goffman, 1969; Berger, Luchman 1966). The former represents groups such as the family, where members share experiences and may have similar values; or the voluntary joining together of a group of friends or co-workers for some shared purpose.

Such groups exist for the benefit of the members of the group. Members are primarily accountable to each other for what occurs within the group. The purpose is largely determined by what the members regard as the group's function, and by what each member wants from the group in terms of personal satisfaction. One family group might see its purpose as creating responsible members of society, living together harmoniously, and helping each other in times of trouble. Another family group might see the provision of material aspects such as providing food, shelter, comfort and the 'good things of life' as its first aim. Similarly, one group of friends might exist only for social reasons – to get together to enjoy themselves. Another might see their function as providing mutual support, sharing ideas, or working together to achieve common goals such as child-minding facilities or better living conditions.

In many naturally occurring groups, however, there may be no overt statement of the group's purpose. Rather there may be a general consensus as to what is done in the group, and members will only remain active within the group so long as they are getting some personal satisfaction out of it.

Created groups are ones where the members have been brought together by someone outside the group, with a particular aim in mind. Groups of this kind would include committees, where members have volunteered to take particular roles or have been elected by others; work groups, where members have been appointed or asked to join; or experimental groups, which have been brought together by a researcher in order to study the workings of a group.

Friendships and partnerships may develop between members of the created group, but these are not the primary purpose of the group. The purpose will have been determined by whoever set up the group. In an experimental group the researcher may not tell the group the real purpose of their being drawn together until the experiment is over, but in most other created groups the purpose and aims are likely to be known by all the members and may be written down or formalized as a kind of blueprint for what the group does and hopes to achieve.

The personal satisfaction that members gain from being in the group may be important as a means of ensuring that they do stay together and co-operate with each other, but achieving the aims and carrying out the task-function of the group may take precedence over ensuring that members' personal needs are met. Created groups are very often accountable to someone outside the group for what they do, how it is to be done, and under what time-scale and conditions.

Within a created group there may be external pressures on the members of the group which make it difficult for members to behave as they would wish. They may have to carry out their roles according to the rules, or they may have to work alongside other group members whom they dislike or would not naturally wish to associate with. Even if they are not gaining satisfaction from being in the group, they may have a duty to remain in it. Members who leave such groups are likely to have to make some kind of formal indication that they are doing so, and, in some cases, may incur penalities if they leave.

For example, someone who has resigned from a committee because he/she does not agree with the committee's perspective or course of action may be debarred from serving on the committee at a future date, or may be stigmatized as a person who is unreliable or difficult to work with. Someone who wants to leave a particular group within the work situation may face unemployment, find it hard to obtain a transfer, or even be denied promotion on the basis of lack of ability to work effectively as one of a team.

Can you differentiate between the created and the naturally occurring Primary Groups of which you are a member? To what extent does your own experience of the purposes and relationships within such groups reflect any of the comments made above?

In analysing the groups on their list some readers may have noted those which occurred naturally for one purpose evolved over time into a group which had a very different function. A group of friends, for example, may initially meet for social purposes but, on finding they have shared interests, may start a club or society of a more formal nature and may invite others to join. As the membership changes, natural groups may also begin to take on characteristics which are more like those of the created group, with formal membership requirements, stated aims and named roles. Similarly, within created groups the development of relationships between members establishes group cohesiveness and gives rise to the kind of voluntary obligations to other members that characterize natural groupings. Thus, in some cases, the distinctions between the two may become blurred and it may be more useful to examine the group in terms of its degree of formality, its task function, roles and relationships, rather than its origins.

Informal Groups

Informal groups are often regarded as leaderless, and purposeless, with no set roles. A closer examination often shows that one person within the group has taken on a leadership role, making suggestions or giving ideas which others are prepared to adopt. Sometimes, too, the role of leader is shared between a number of people, with different people taking the lead on different occasions.

The person who emerges as a leader in an informal group may be someone with a strong, dominant personality, the ability to produce ideas to which the group can relate, and the communication skill to persuade others to go along with the course of action suggested. Or the leader in the group may be someone who is seen to have more power, status or knowledge than the others. Alternatively the leader may be the most popular person in the group, the one with whom everyone feels at ease, or the one who seems to embody the ideals of the group. These ideals could represent anything from style of dress and speech, to intellectual ability or toughness and street credibility.

In groups where the leadership role is shared among the group members there is likely to be the kind of homogeneity in the group which makes it difficult for a single individual to stand out from the others. But even in informal groups where there is a clearly identified leader, homogeneity tends to be a feature of the membership. The members may be of the same sex or the same race, come from a similar area or strata of society, be part of the same organization or have strong interests in common. This homogeneity helps create solidarity within the group and can be useful when the group is trying to get things done. There is less likelihood of dissent and therefore more chance that decisions arrived at will be carried out and supported by all. However, homogeneous groups may lack the breadth of perspective that can be achieved in more mixed groups. Homogeneity can lead to prejudice and it may be very difficult for someone who is not of the same race, religion, etc. to join and be accepted. There can also be a danger of sectarianism which leads to rivalry between groups.

In addition to leader roles, other roles may be detected within informal groups. For example, some people within a group may be naturally passive, content always to take the role of followers or supporters of those who lead. Others may not be leaders but habitually be active in the group. There may be some people who take a very peripheral role, joining the group or taking part in its activities only on an occasional basis. There may also be people who regularly join in the group but who are not fully accepted by others and who remain in the role of isolates, with no real friends within the group. Sometimes these isolates become the butt of group jokes, performing the role of scapegoat for the group and being tolerated for their amusement value. Other people may take on the role of group clown – the person who is expected to make jokes or cheer up the others. Other group roles may include the morale builder – the person who can always be relied on to make others feel good – the peacemaker, or the dissenter who creates arguments or tensions within the group.

Even though the group operates in an informal way members may communicate quite clearly, either in words, actions or by non-verbal signals, what kind of behaviour is expected and what is not acceptable within the group. Conformity to group norms and expectations is often a major feature of such groups and, as we saw in Chapter Two, those who do not conform may find it difficult to gain group acceptance. Someone, for example, who normally drinks very little alcohol may find, in a group of social drinkers, that there is a need to conform by buying rounds and drinking more than usual. Another person may have to adopt a rather different style of dress to gain acceptance within a group.

Informal groups often develop their own style of language, with particular words acting as a sort of jargon, the meaning of which is obvious only to those in the group. Conformity with the conventions of language within the group may be a condition for group acceptance.

> **Can you identify the 'unwritten rules' in any of the informal groups of which you are a member? Are there any language or dress conventions within the group? Does it have its own jargon? How strong is the pressure to conform, and in what kind of ways do you conform? Do you do so because you identify with the values of the group or because you want to gain acceptance or remain a member, or for some other reason?**
>
> **Have you ever refused to conform to the norms of an informal group of which you were a member? What was the outcome, and why?**

Many people conform with group norms because they genuinely share the same values and interests as other members of the group. Others conform simply to be part of the group. It is usually only those who are on the periphery of the group, or dominant leader-type individuals who can be non-conformist and still remain members.

A particularly striking example of an informal group which has developed strict conventions of behaviour is the gang. There is usually a clearly defined leader, or group of leaders. Those wishing to join the gang must be seen to fit, and their loyalty to the gang's ideals may be tested before they are fully accepted. They may, for example, have to demonstrate solidarity in defending the group against others, or in carrying out a task which demonstrates their credibility.

An account of juvenile street gangs in Glasgow in the 1970s, provides examples of the type of rules and conventions operating within this kind of informal group. Despite the best efforts of social workers and police it proved impossible to lessen the group solidarity. Threats, promises and offers of help were all ineffective in breaking down group conformity. It was only when the gang leaders were arrested that it became possible to effect changes of behaviour and different norms within the groups (Patrick, 1973).

When students talk about 'our gang' they are generally referring to a much less extreme grouping than the street gang but many of the same characteristics may be seen, albeit in a more pro-social rather than anti-social form!

> **Have you ever referred to 'our crowd' or 'our gang' when talking about a group of which you were a member? If so, how were the conventions and rules of behaviour communicated within your 'gang' and what did you say or do to exclude those who were not acceptable as members? What did you gain, at the personal level, from being one of the crowd?**

Even though informal groups may not have an overtly stated purpose, members of group usually know what they hope to gain from their involvement in the group. They may wish to make friends or alleviate loneliness, to meet members of the opposite sex or people with the same interests, or to persuade the others to adopt a particular course of action. They may see membership of the group as conferring status, or helping them in their career as a result of meeting the right people.

To say that a group is informal, therefore, does not mean that the group lacks rules or roles. It does mean that these are determined by convention within the group and may not be immediately apparent to an outsider who has not studied the group closely.

Formal Groups

Formal groups are more clearly defined. They usually have an identifiable leader or role structure, rules are often stated overtly, the purpose of the group is clearly formulated and group meetings are generally arranged for a specific time and place – often on a regular basis. Conformity with the rules may be a stated condition of group membership rather than a matter of convention.

Although members of a formal group may have clearly defined roles such as leader, treasurer, recorder, etc., they may also adopt many of the roles which occur in the informal group. Other groups may be formalized only to the extent that the group has a designated leader and a very definite task to perform, with other roles and inter-actions being more informally determined.

Formal groups often have a defined membership quota – for example six committee members or a working party of twelve. In theory anyone who complies with the conditions of membership may be eligible to join if there is a place available. In practice it may be necessary to be elected. The chances of being elected may be dependent on other qualities such as age, status, popularity, etc., which have nothing to do with the formal conditions of membership.

The leader of a formal group may also have to undertake specific duties such as setting up and chairing group meetings, and ensuring that the group carries out its duties as specified in the rules. Where the leader, and those in other named roles such as treasurer or secretary, have been elected by the membership they are accountable to the members for their conduct. In most formal groups these roles are held for a finite period and members either have to seek re-elec-tion or have to step down once this period is up. Re-election may be dependent on whether the roles have been performed to the satisfac-tion of other members, and on whether there are others, equally or more acceptable, who are making a bid to take over the roles.

In groups where the leader, or others, have been appointed by an outside agency, accountability can be more of a problem. There may be a need to ensure that the needs of group members are met in order that the group can remain cohesive and effective. The need to comply with external conditions may make it difficult for the leader to satisfy these conditions and, at the same time, meet the needs of individual group members.

For example, the leader of a project group at work may find that the group wants to take time to discuss and analyse a problem in great depth. A refusal to allow this could lead to feelings of resent-ment or frustration among group members. At the same time the leader may be aware that those further up the organizational hier-archy are pushing for a speedy answer to the problem. If the leader doesn't deliver in time it is she who is seen to be responsible for the group's failure to deliver. But if she pushes the group to make a quick decision it is she who will have to live with the consequences in the group of members' negative feelings. This may also reduce her power in the group and make it difficult, on a subsequent occasion, to gain group cohesion and solidarity in carrying out a plan of action which she has suggested.

The management theorist, John Adair (1979, 1984), has written at some length on the subject of leader accountability within both formal and informal groups. He suggests that in any group which has a clear task function the leader of the group will have to try to balance up the needs of the individual members with the needs of the group and the demands of the task itself. The more overlap there is between the needs of the three, the more likely it is that the group will perform amicably and effectively. It is up to the leader to try to identify or create these areas of overlap.

What a leader does in order to balance out the three areas of need will depend to a great extent on the personal leadership style and the communication ability of the leader.

Leadership Styles

One classification of leadership styles, which is still widely quoted in management texts, is that devised by the psychologist Kurt Lewin in the late 1940s. This classification distinguishes four types of leader – autocratic, democratic, bureaucratic and *laissez-faire*.

In its most extreme form, the autocratic or authoritarian leader is one who is conscious of the need to maintain a distance between himself and his followers in order that his authority may be obeyed. He expects to issue orders and to have them carried out. He does not see the need for consultation but regards it as part of his leadership role to take decisions and to ensure that they are acted upon. He will generally supervise his followers closely to make sure that they do carry out orders and will see it as his duty to censure those who do not perform effectively. Such a leader may be task-oriented – more concerned with getting the job done than with the feelings of those in the group.

Leaders of this type can often inspire considerable loyalty among their followers, and, because they do get things done, may be admired both by those outside the group and by group members themselves. On the negative side, authoritarian leadership may result in followers who will not work unless closely supervised, who are unwilling or afraid to put forward ideas, who become resentful of lack of consultation, or who passively wait for instructions rather than acting on their own initiative. When the leader is absent the group may be unable to function effectively.

> **Can you think of any group leaders you have known who could be described as authoritarian? Was their behaviour as extreme as that outlined above? What effect did their leadership have on the group?**

At the opposite extreme is the democratic or corporate leader. He will try to create a feeling of rapport between himself and followers. He will want followers to participate in decision-making and to discuss plans and agree to them before they are implemented. Such leaders are often referred to as morale-oriented as they will be concerned to create good morale, co-operation, solidarity and cohesiveness within their group and will believe that tasks performed under such conditions are likely to be done with more effectiveness and enthusiasm.

Under leaders of this type tasks may be performed more slowly because time is taken up by consultation and discussion. If, however, the leader is absent the group is likely to function quite effectively and to be motivated to do the task well without a need for constant, close supervision. The group may also find more pleasure in the work because they feel personally involved.

Have you any experience of a democratic leader? How did you react to this form of leadership?

Bureaucratic leaders are ones who gain their authority by 'going by the book'. They often tend towards authoritarianism but will not take risks in case they trangress the rules. Groups who have to operate under this form of leadership may find that they are hedged around by restrictions and have to pay considerable attention to doing things the 'correct' way rather than in a new way or in the most productive way.

Laissez-faire is not so much a leadership style as a lack of leadership. A *laissez-faire* leader simply lets things happen – neither gathering the group together for consultation, nor imposing authority. If the group goes ahead and gets on with things – fine! If not, such a leader is unlikely to push for action and the group may feel that it has no leader. When this occurs other individuals within the group may take over the leadership role and there may be general tensions and power struggles within the group as a result of the lack of leadership.

Bureaucratic and *laissez-faire* leadership are perhaps less common but you may have encountered leaders of this type. How did you and other members of the group react to them and what were the advantages and disadvantages of their leadership?

The various leadership styles outlined above have been given in their most extreme form and few leaders will conform exactly to type. What tends to happen is that individuals have one preferred style but are able to adapt their style when the occasion demands it. An autocratic leader, for example, may recognize that there are times when it is necessary to consult, while a democratic leader may, if time is short and things have to be done in a hurry, become more authoritarian. Sometimes, within a group there will be an official leader who is fairly authoritarian and task-oriented, and an unofficial or deputy leader who makes it his function to keep up morale and see to it that the individual needs of members are met.

Other writers have suggested additional leadership types – the leader from behind, who does not appear to exert leadership or impose his views but who is able to manipulate the group to do what he wants; the personality-oriented leader, who relies on popularity and the likeableness of his personality to persuade others to follow him; the supportive leader, who is so attentive to the personal needs of his group that they feel it would be churlish to do anything but support him in return; and the helpless leader, who appeals to the protective instinct in the group and gets things done because the group doesn't want to see him in trouble (Handy, 1978; Pfeiffer & Goodstein, 1984).

Communication in Groups

There is a natural tendency to assume that an authoritarian leader will bark out orders, while a democratic leader will adopt a more gentle, persuasive form of speech. While this may be true in some cases the way in which leaders and followers communicate is likely to be much less stereotyped and more varied.

One method for analysing group communication is Bales' Interaction Process analysis. This gives a list of behaviours such as: shows solidarity; asks for information; gives opinion; disagrees; shows tension release, etc. It is particularly useful for analysing a group discussion. When an individual engages in one of the behaviours shown an observer puts a tick against that aspect. Each observer studies only one person in the group and, with practice, observers can be trained to be very quick and accurate in ticking the behaviours shown. Subsequent analysis allows the participants in the discussion to discover whether they were hogging the conversation, giving helpful suggestions or being negative. This knowledge can help the individual to develop a more balanced and effective range of responses.

> **Can you devise a simple checklist which would enable you to analyse the communication and interaction of individuals within a group? If you are working on your own you could try using your schedule to analyse a group discussion on radio or TV. Bales' schedule is contained in his book which is referenced at the end of this chapter. You might find it interesting to compare your categories with those he suggests.**

Another scheme for analysing group behaviour has been developed by De Bono (1985). In his book *Six thinking hats* he suggests that when we employ different kinds of thinking it is as if we were wearing a different hat. He uses this analogy to provide a number of exercises which will allow those who habitually look on the negative side to take a more positive view, to help the optimists be more realistic, to encourage creative ideas in those who find this difficult, and to provide a means whereby those who operate emotionally rather than rationally may learn to take account of facts.

Another theorist who has helped our understanding of group processes is the psychotherapist Moreno. In the 1950s he invented a technique called sociometry for examining the patterns of roles within a group. The technique is a simple one in which people within a group are asked to respond to one or two specific questions such as: 'who do you think is the best person to lead this group?'; who would you like to have as your best friend?'; 'who would you most like to work with?', etc. By plotting out the answers on a sociogram it is possible to see what the interactions are in a group, who the leaders or most popular people are, and who are the isolates who need to be integrated. Each arrow represents an individual's choice and, as can be seen in the diagram below, this group contains two isolates, several pairs of friends, and a small group of people who cluster around one individual.

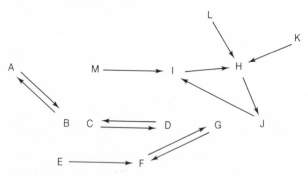

Fig 7.1

Sociograms of this kind have been used in education and work settings to try to achieve effective groups for project work and to help isolates become integrated. They have also been used in institutions for disturbed or delinquent adolescents in order to try to create a social mix which is pleasing to the individuals and, at the same time, likely to encourage more pro-social behaviour and a greater degree of cohesion between inmates and staff.

Transactional Analysis

In Chapter Six we saw how Berne's theory of TA provides one explanation for the different types of role behaviour that individuals habitually engage in – the need to obtain either positive or negative strokes in order to reaffirm one's sense of self. Another aspect of TA theory provides an explanation for some of the communication difficulties which occur between individuals and between leaders and followers in groups.

Berne suggests that each act of communication can be seen as a transaction in which one person trades off strokes with another. In addition each of us has three possible modes of behaviour, any one of which we may employ in communicating with others. These three modes of behaviour – Berne refers to them as ego-states – may be regarded as the adult state, the parent state or the child state. They are not indicators of age or parental status, but rather descriptors of particular role behaviour which can be observed and analysed in our communication.

The child state may take one of three forms: the curious, receptive, wondering, dependent and enthusiastic child; the stubborn, rebellious, naughty child; or the adapted child who always tries to please. Each of us will, on occasion, and regardless of our age, display the kind of behaviour we learned as children. And there may be times when it is entirely appropriate to do so. Someone who is 90 years old may, for example, may show the enthusiasm and curiosity of a child when encountering a new and pleasant experience. But if someone behaves like a sulky child when asked to perform a task at work this is likely to be both inappropriate and unproductive. Sometimes, however, we find ourselves responding like children because someone else has adopted a parental tone and is treating us like children.

The parent state is one which is modelled on our own parents, or adults who influenced us in our formative years. Again this may take several forms: the supportive, nurturing parent; the critical disapproving parent; the teaching or the preaching parent. When we are operating in parent mode we may very well find ourselves using a turn of phrase or tone of voice which is reminiscent of the way parent figures spoke to us. Again, there may be times when it is appropriate to operate in this mode – for example, when being supportive to a friend in need, or when giving advice to someone who asks for it. But leaders who treat their followers as if they were naughty children shouldn't be too surprised if their followers rebel, and do so in a singularly childish manner.

Both the parent and child states are essentially emotional. The adult state is one in which reason is employed, rather than emotion. It is characterized by logical argument, reasoned discussion and a reliance on obtaining the appropriate facts and information of a situation before coming to a decision on it. When someone wants us to be enthusiastic and emotional the adult state is unlikely to be seen as an appropriate response. But when something needs to be discussed and reasoned out the adult state is likely to be the most productive one.

Consider the following pieces of dialogue. Which state – adult, parent or child – does each exemplify?

1 John, haven't you finished that piece of work yet? It seems to be taking you ages. I've asked you for it several times and you just don't seem to care that I need it.

2 John, could you do me a favour and type this out for me? Please? I don't like to ask you, but I'm going to be in real trouble if I haven't got it for tomorrow.

3 John, do you have a moment free some time today when we could discuss the Morrison file? The deadline's getting close and I'm a bit concerned in case we don't get it done in time. Perhaps we could get together and try to sort out what's the best approach?

In the first example the parental state was likely to result in John's responding like a child – 'Do it yourself if it's so important!' Or, if he didn't respond in that kind of language – perhaps because he had too much at stake to risk doing so – he might have felt like a small boy who has been shouted at by his father and react inwardly as he did in youth. On the other hand, he might have wanted to respond in an adult way and in order to do so he would have to rein in his emotions and not be goaded into a childish response.

In the second example the tone is that of the wheedling child – 'please let me stay up late'; 'please can I have a toffee?'; 'please don't let them hurt me!' John might well respond to this by feeling parental and responsible, and rush happily to get the job done. Alternatively, he might feel he was being manipulated and resist the pressure to obey, pointing out in an adult way the reasons why he couldn't drop everything at that moment to help the other out. He might even respond with a childish tit for tat – 'No, why should I help you? You didn't help me last week.'

In the final example John is being invited to engage in adult discussion in order to solve the problem. The most likely response would be an adult one. If John responded in either child or parent mode this might provoke the other to abandon the adult approach and the conversation might degenerate into an argument.

Berne describes these different reaction in terms of either crossed or complementary transactions as shown in the models below.

When people voluntarily operate in a complementary mode conversation flows and both people are getting the kind of stroking they want from each other. This does not mean the conversation will be free from emotion or strife. In fact any parent/parent, child/child, or child/parent transaction will have emotional overtones, and sometimes these will be negative emotions. When the mode is adult/adult there will be a lack of emotion and no perceived need for stroking by either party. Again, conversation is likely to flow easily between them.

Crossed transactions, on the other hand, not only create emotional tensions but very often lead to strong negative feelings, harsh

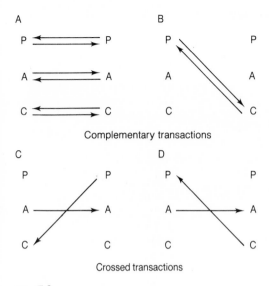

Complementary transactions

Crossed transactions

Fig 7.2

words or attempts at appeasement and may lead to a breakdown in communication, with both parties feeling misunderstood and aggrieved.

> The piece of dialogue which follows is an example of a transaction which becomes progressively more crossed. Can you analyse the various states represented in it?
>
> Leader: John, could I see you for a moment later today to discuss the Morrison file?
>
> John: Don't talk to me about the Morrison file! I'm fed up looking at it.
>
> Leader: You may be fed up looking at it but you don't seem to have done much about it.
>
> John: Oh really? And who said I was responsible for it? I don't see anyone else rushing to help.
>
> Leader: It's your responsibility. You know that. Anyway, you're the one who insisted that I delegate more. Fat lot of good that's done me.
>
> John: Oh, don't tell me you delegated it because I wanted it. You delegated because you didn't want to do it.
>
> Leader: Look John, we're getting nowhere like this. Couldn't we just sit down and discuss it reasonably?
>
> John . . .
>
> When you have analysed the transactions given try continuing the dialogue from the leader's final line, perhaps introducing others who will react in adult, parent or child modes also.

TA is currently becoming popular within firms as a way of helping employees – particularly team leaders and those who have to co-operate in groups – to understand why communication sometimes goes wrong. A disapproving or hectoring parental tone may provoke an emotional childish reaction even if the words themselves are innocuous enough. Someone who is simply trying to be assertive may adopt the tone of a belligerent child and sound aggressive, making it less likely that others will respond pleasantly and easily. Someone who is always rational, always adult, never showing emotion, may dampen enthusiasm in others or create a working climate which is all work and no play and therefore dull.

Group Cohesion, Solidarity and Groupthink

In this chapter we have referred several times to the need for groups to achieve cohesion and solidarity if they are to perform effectively. Research has shown that cohesive groups do tend to perform more effectively and be more satisfying for the members (Austin & Worchel, 1979). There is, however, a danger in too much cohesion within a group, especially if the group also has a strong, dominant and respected leader. The danger is that the group will engage in what has been termed 'groupthink' (Janis, 1972).

In a group which perceives itself as a cohesive, effective and successful unit, communication will be aimed towards minimizing conflict and maintaining cohesion. Since non-conformity might damage the cohesion, members who privately disagree with the views expressed by the leader, and supported by the majority, may be unwilling to risk conflict by publicly admitting that they disagree.

President Kennedy's decision to invade Cuba in 1961 was a good example of this. No one in his circle of close advisers disagreed publicly with his decision. When interviewed later, when the invasion had been unsuccessful and things had gone very badly for the US, many of the advisers admitted that they had disagreed privately but had been unwilling to express disagreement for fear of creating conflicts in a group which was generally close and cohesive.

This willingness to suppress disagreement and conform to the leader's view is one aspect of groupthink. Another is the feeling of security and superiority that may come from group solidarity. This may result in the group's being prepared to take chances which others might consider unwise or too risky. Or the group may be persuaded to take risks by a strong leader who regards himself or herself as adventurous and enterprising. This is referred to as the 'risky shift' in which the group shifts towards bolder, more adventurous behaviour (Myers & Myers, 1982). This may explain why a street gang, for example, will engage in more violent activity than the individual members do outside the gang.

Other cohesive groups may favour the 'cautious shift'. This tends to occur in groups where the members wish to be seen to have a social conscience and where the decisions of the group might affect those weaker than themselves. In this situation the group may opt for a more cautious course of action than individual members might advocate if deciding on their own (Brown, 1986).

Summary

Regardless of whether it is formal or informal, naturally occurring or created, the small Primary group can be regarded as a dynamic, self-contained system with a clearly defined boundary. It comprises three elements – inputs, process and outputs.

The INPUTS are all those aspects which contribute towards the composition of the group. These may be *personal* – the feelings, aims, motivation, roles and relationships among individual group members. They may be *structural* – the size and homogeneity of the group, the duration and timing of group meetings, and the location in which the group meets. Or they may be *task-oriented* – the reason for the group's formation, what it hopes to achieve, and whether the group task is self-imposed or determined by someone outwith the group.

The PROCESS is the method whereby individuals within the group communicate – who talks to whom, and for what purpose.

OUTPUTS may be the tangible outcomes of the group's effort – products produced, problems solved or aims achieved. Or they may be the effects on the group members of their interaction with each other. Both types of output provide feedback to members of the group about communication and relationships within the group, and about how well the group is performing. This feedback modifies the inputs and this, in turn, may have an effect on subsequent outputs and processes within the group.

But, of course, few groups can operate entirely as small self-contained units. Even the most tightly-knit family group is subject to influences from the external environment in which it operates. It is these external influences which we consider in the next chapter, when we look at primary groups as units within a larger system – the organization – and examine the ways in which the communication and behaviour of individuals and groups is affected by their roles and tasks within an organizational structure.

REFERENCES

ADAIR, J. (1979): *Action-centred leadership*. Gower

—— (1984): *The skills of leadership*. Gower

ARGYLE, M. (1983): *Social interaction*. Methuen

AUSTIN, W.G. & WORCHEL, S. (eds) (1979): *The social psychology of intergroup relations*. Brooks-Cole

BALES, R.F. (1950): *Interaction process analysis*. Addison-Wesley

BERGER, P. & LUCHMAN, T. (1966): *The social construction of reality*. Doubleday

BERNE, E. (1966): *Games people play*. Deutsch

BROWN, R. (1986): *Social psychology*. The Free Press

CARTWRIGHT, D. & ZANDER, A. (1953): *Group dynamics: research and theory*. Tavistock

COOLEY, C. (1909): *Social organization*. Scribner

DE BONO, E. (1985): *Six thinking hats*. Viking Press

EISNER, J.R. (1986): *Social psychology*. Sage

GOFFMAN, E. (1969): *The presentation of self in everyday life*. Penguin

HANDY, C. (1978): *The gods of management*. Souvenir Press

HARE, A.P. (1962): *Handbook of small group research*. The Free Press

JANIS, I.L. (1972): *Victims of group think*; Houghton Mifflin

LEWIN, K. (1948): *Resolving social conflicts*. Harper & Row

—— (1951): *Field theory in social science*. Harper & Row

MAIER, N.R.F. (1970): *Problem-solving and creativity in individuals and groups*. Brooks-Cole

MORENO, T.L. (1953): *Who shall survive?* Beacon

MYERS, M.T. & MYERS, G.E. (1982): *Managing communication: an organizational approach*. McGraw-Hill

PATRICK, J. (1973): *A Glasgow gang observed*. Methuen

PFEIFFER, J.W. & GOODSTEIN, L.D. (1984): *The 1984 annual: developing human resources*. University Associates Inc.

TAJFEL, F. & FRASER, C. (1986): *Introducing social psychology*. Pelican

THOMAS, E.J. (1967): *Behavioural science for social workers*. The Free Press

CHAPTER EIGHT

COMMUNICATION IN ORGANIZATIONS

In the previous chapter we looked at patterns of interaction and communication within small groups. In this chapter we turn our attention to larger systems – the organizations in which we spend much of our working lives.

If we think of an organization as comprising a number of individuals and groups each of whom affects or is affected by the others, and the organization itself as a system which influences and is influenced by factors outside the system, it becomes obvious that organizational communication will have a considerable degree of complexity.

We are concerned not only with who talks to whom and for what purpose within the organization, but also with

- how groups interact and influence each other;
- how the organization is regarded by those outside it;
- how the organization communicates with those outside it;
- who holds leadership or power roles in the organization;
- how other roles are determined;
- how information about performance is conveyed;
- the system of threats or rewards in operation;
- the nature, aims and objectives of the organization;
- the organizational structure and culture.

The nature of the organization will have an effect on factors like the homogeneity and size of groups, where they are located, the buildings they occupy and the tools they use. The organization's aims, and who determines these aims, will have a bearing on the extent to which individuals are satisfied with the organization and identify with its goals. The culture of an organization is determined by the way in which all these factors integrate to produce an accepted set of norms, conventions and values which will be slightly different within every organization.

Why Do People Join Organizations?

List all the factors which influenced you to join the university or other organization of which you are a member. List the factors which you find satisfying in the organization.

List those which cause you dissatisfaction or might make you consider leaving.

Prioritize the factors on your list by noting whether each is either crucial, very important, important, or not very important to you as a source of influence, satisfaction or dissatisfaction.

Compare your lists and note whether there are any common factors and how you have prioritized them. If you are working with others, compare lists and discuss the reasons for any similarities or differences noted.

The psychologist Herzberg (1966) has suggested that the factors which motivate us to join an organization, or to remain within it, are not the same as those which give rise to satisfaction with the organization. He argues that material factors such as location, ease of transportation or accommodation, reputation, pay, hours, holidays and conditions of service are the kind of factors which influence us in joining an organization. Similar factors may give rise to dissatisfaction with the organization and may encourage us to look elsewhere. If, however, these factors are not a cause for dissatisfaction, there is no guarantee that we will feel satisfied. Herzberg argues that satisfaction arises out of a quite different set of factors such as the interest and challenge in the work itself, personal achievement, the possibility of future advancement, and a feeling that one is liked, respected or admired by superiors and colleagues.

How well does Herzberg's theory stand up in relation to your lists? Do you believe that the material aspects are or are not sufficient to create satisfaction? Why?

Expectancy Theory

Several theorists have argued that they have been unable to replicate Herzberg's findings and that his theory has not been sufficiently proved (Vroom, 1967; Porter & Lawler, 1968). They suggest that what motivates is expectation about what will happen, and what satisfies or dissatisfies is the differential between what we expect to happen and what actually does happen. If we expect a positive outcome from a course of action we will be motivated to undertake it. A negative expectation will have the opposite effect. And we compare different courses of action on the basis of our expectation of the outcomes of them.

A student who joined a particular university with high expectations about the swinging social life might be dissatisfied if there was little social life, or if the work-load was so high that it was impossible to take advantage of the social life without failing all the exams! A person who joined a firm because the money was good and the job likely to be no worse than the present job may feel considerable satisfaction when the job turns out better than expected.

Both of these theories have implications for job interviews. What is said to the candidate in the initial interview may set up expectations which could, if not realized, lead to job dissatisfaction; while seeking a job which provides good material benefits may not necessarily provide job satisfaction.

The argument that satisfaction may come as a result of being given recognition, respect or liking by colleagues and superiors has implications for managerial communication. It is similar to Berne's concept of positive stroking which was discussed in Chapter Six. It also relates to the 'halo' effect and the 'self-fulfilling' prophecy mentioned in Chapter Two. An individual who believes himself to be well thought of by others is not only likely to have a better opinion of himself, but is also likely to work harder and perform to a higher standard.

The manager who fails to provide a word of praise, recognition or encouragement when staff have done a good job may be paving the way for worker dissatisfaction and poorer performance in the longer term. The phatic communication discussed in Chapter Three is one of the devices which people in organizations may use to ensure that there is a feeling of mutual regard and recognition. A brief comment about the bad weather may be all that is needed to brighten up the day and reassure others that they are recognized as people and not simply units of production.

Studies carried out in the 1920s in the Hawthorne factory of the Western Electric Company in America showed that the productivity of workers rose when their area of the work-place was better lit. When the lighting was reduced productivity still continued to rise (Mayo, 1933)! It was concluded that the rise in productivity had little to do with the lighting conditions and everything to do with the fact that people knew they were involved in a scientific experiment, enjoyed the novelty and felt special as a result. The 'Hawthorne Effect' led researchers to treat the results of experiments with caution and to discount those positive effects which might simply be the result of people's positive feelings about being involved.

However, more recent theorists have come to regard the principles behind the Hawthorne Effect as a motivating device – find ways of keeping some interesting novelty in the work, let people see that you are taking an interest in them, and encourage members of an organization to take pride in their membership and to feel that it is rather special. Creating these conditions may result in a satisfied workforce and increase the overal productivity of the firm (Rickards, 1985; Majaro, 1988).

To what extent do you believe that communication and motivating devices such as recognition, stroking, phatic communication are:

1 A cynical attempt to manipulate the workforce into making the firm more profitable for its owners or shareholders?

2 A sensible means of creating job satisfaction and a good working environment within an organization?

Consider the pros and cons of the two points of view.

One of the major objections to many of these motivation and communication principles is the fact that some people do consider them to be manipulative. On the other hand, many of the most successful companies – and ones in which there appears to be little industrial unrest – employ these communication techniques as a matter of course (Naisbitt, 1986). Perhaps one reason why they work is because they answer some of the human needs which other psychologists have suggested are essential for human satisfaction.

Needs Theories

In the 1940s Maslow put forward a theory which has had considerable influence ever since. He suggested that human beings are motivated to take a particular course of action in order to satisfy basic human needs. These needs operate in a hierarchical way. When one level of need has been satisfied, another set of needs surfaces and requires to be met. At the most basic level are physiological survival needs – the need to satisfy hunger, obtain shelter and reproduce the species. People who are in dire poverty may not have any choice about which organization they will join. They either take the job that is available or adopt some other course of action that enables them to survive.

If, however, basic survival needs are being satisfied, the second level of needs surface. These needs are the ones we discussed earlier. They relate to companionship and belonging, status and the need for recognition and liking. People who are operating at this level of need will feel more satisfied within an organization where they feel valued and which gives them job security and a feeling of involvement. Sometimes people who regard their job as a means of satisfying survival needs will join other organizations in their spare time in order to satisfy needs for belonging and recognition.

When this level of need is being satisfied the final level of needs arises. These are the self-actualizing needs that we mentioned in the last chapter – the need to find interest and stimulation, challenge and responsibility, to take risks, try new ventures and be in control of our own lives. People with such needs will tend to join organizations which are not rigidly controlled, which encourage enterprise and initiative, and in which it is possible to do interesting and challenging work. Again, if these needs cannot be met within the work situation, the individual may seek to meet them in leisure occupations or within other social organizations.

Other psychologists, McClelland & Winteer (1969), suggested that needs come into one of three categories – the need for achievement, the need for power, or the need for affiliation. Which needs will be dominant will depend on the personality of the individual. Some people will have strong needs in all three areas and may have to satisfy the different needs in different aspects of life. This could lead to role conflicts of the type described in Chapter Six.

People with a high need for achievement may look for a job in an organization that has good promotion prospects and gives opportunities for individuals to succeed. The person with a high need for power may try to find work in an organization like the armed forces or the civil service, which are bound by rules and operate in a way which allows people to exercise a degree of power. Affiliation needs are the belonging needs already discussed.

You may have noted that several of the theories mentioned above are based on research carried out in the 1960s. One reason for this is that the 1960s represented a time of growth and change in industrial and social organizations. The effects of the Second World War were beginning to recede. People were looking forward to the future. There were considerable advances in technology – especially the technology of communication. Better road, rail and air links made travel between countries easier, and more efficient methods of information transmission provided the means for improved communication both within and between organizations.

New markets were opening up and the general trend in business organizations was to try to achieve growth. Better access to information allowed comparison between different organizations and gave rise to questions like: why is Firm A more successful than Firm B? Why are the workers in Firm C more satisfied? Are there newer, different and more effective ways of organizing things? Occupational and social psychologists carried out research which tried to answers these questions, and the term 'organizational culture' was coined to describe the environment which operated within different organizational systems (Blake & Mouton, 1964; Watson, 1963; Drucker, 1974).

Organizational Culture

Look at the 20 statements below and give each a rating from 1 to 5 according to whether you
   1 – strongly agree
   2 – agree
   3 – neither agree nor disagree
   4 – disagree
   5 – strongly disagree.
1 On the whole, I do not like to exert myself.
2 I generally work hard at things I am asked to do.

3 I avoid responsibility.
4 I enjoy having responsibility.
5 I am not particularly interested in achievement.
6 I have a strong desire to achieve.
7 I like to be told what to do.
8 I prefer to decide for myself what I will do.
9 I find it difficult to make decisions.
10 I find decision-making fairly easy.
11 I tend not to work unless there is a good reason.
12 I do not find it difficult to motivate myself to work.
13 If I didn't need the money I wouldn't take a job.
14 I'd be bored if I couldn't find interesting work to do.
15 I'd work harder if the boss was watching.
16 I generally try to do a job to the best of my ability.
17 I'd work harder if I was offered more money.
18 Interesting work is more important to me than high pay.
19 I'm quite happy to let others do the work without me.
20 I like the help and support of others when I work.

The statements above are also based on theories of human motivation put forward in the 1960s (McGregor, 1960). The first theory, 'Theory X', is that human beings are basically passive, feel more secure when they are told what to do, and need a system of rewards or threats in order to motivate them to work. 'Theory Y' takes the opposite view – that human beings are active, information-seeking creatures who are capable of self-determination and responsible behaviour. Theory X predicts that people work only to obtain the necessities or luxuries of life. Theory Y suggests that, even if we were comfortably rich without working, we would still be driven to find interesting things to do in order to avoid boredom and find satisfaction.

> **If you scored mostly 3s in the test above you obviously didn't want to commit yourself to either theory! If you scored 1s and 2s in most of the odd-numbered statements, you tend towards Theory X. If you scored 1s and 2s in most of the even-numbered statements your view is nearer that of Theory Y.**

We suspect that readers might favour Theory Y when faced with bald statements like those in the test above. But for many years, in both Britain and America, the popular view of workers within organizations was that of Theory X. Hence the need for clocking-in to ensure that people didn't come in late or go off early, shop-floor supervision to make sure that people were gainfully employed, bonus payments to increase productivity, and autocratic management which outlined exactly what had to be done, and the procedures to be adopted in doing it.

The culture and communication patterns within a Theory X organization will be very different from those in a Theory Y organization. An X manager will assume that workers do not want responsibility or participation in decision-making, and will take personal responsibility for most of the planning, organizing and controlling of work within the organization. The organization is likely to be structured hierarchically, with most of the power concentrated at the top. It may be assumed that workers do not require much information, and any information that they do need may be fed down to them in the form of instructions or directives. Since it is assumed that pay is the most important motivator, there may be less attention paid to the conditions under which workers have to operate.

This rather extreme Theory X orientation has not been confined to industrial organizations. Many educational establishments took a similar view – hence the emphasis on assessments as a means of making students attend classes and do the necessary work, and lectures structured to inform rather than invite discussion. In hospitals the X view assumes that patients do not need to be given explanation or invited to discuss their case, merely be given instructions which will be in their best interest. While civil servants and local authorities with an X orientation will assume that their clients are passive and accepting – perhaps trying to get as much as they can out of the system without having to work for it!

This view gives rise to a 'them and us' attitude and may lead to feelings of frustration. It can produce confrontation between management and workers and lead to industrial unrest, with workers perceiving a need for strong unions to protect their interests.

Another study carried out in 1960s suggested that it was possible to detect two distinct types of organizational system – the mechanistic and organic (Burns & Stalker, 1962). The mechanistic system has a culture influenced by Theory X. Burns and Stalker found that successful organizations in established industries, and within a market environment where demand was relatively stable, tend to be mechanistic. Newer companies, especially those which produce innovative products within a more dynamic and competitive market environment, have to be more flexible and responsive to change. Companies in this situation tend to be more successful when they adopt an organic structure based on Theory Y.

The manager within an organic system will think of employees as having a great deal of potential to become interested and motivated in the job and will see the managerial role as one which seeks to find ways of realizing that potential for the good of the individual and the organization. Co-operation, rather than confrontation, will be seen as the way forward. Breaking down traditional 'them and us' attitudes will be a necessary stage in this process and managerial behaviour will be geared towards getting employees involved in planning, in problem-solving and in taking personal responsibility for their own work.

If 'growth' was the keyword of the 1960s 'enterprise' is that of the 1980s and beyond. There have been so many technological and social changes over the last decade, that many of the established industries have declined. The service industries and the new electronic industries which have taken their place are operating in the kind of dynamic and competitive environment which calls for a flexible response to marketing and planning. If companies want to succeed they may have to take calculated risks and be open to new ideas. The success of Japanese firms has created interest in their management principles which are much more akin to those of Theory Y (Handy, 1988).

More organizations are now moving towards a culture with a Y orientation. In these organizations the need for good organizational communication at all levels becomes crucial. Workers cannot make decisions unless they have access to relevant information. Managers cannot know what the workforce thinks or feels unless there is some forum for consultation. There may be a need to identify and reward – either by promotion, more challenging work or more money – the enterprising and creative individuals who will seek out new markets, suggest more effective methods of operation, or provide innovative and creative ideas for new products, planning or budgeting methods.

Communication methods such as appraisal and counselling interviews will enable the firm to identify these individuals. Groups such as quality circles (which will be discussed later) can provide a forum for communication and the emergence of new ideas. To feed ideas back from workers to management there will be a need for upward as well as downward communication flow. In order that sections of the workforce will not be operating in a way that is contrary to the general interest, there will also be a need for lateral communication flow among all the various groups and individuals at any one level. Indeed, the whole concept of 'level', and the need for a hierarchy of authority, may be one which requires rethinking in organizations where the culture is strongly influenced by a Theory Y orientation.

Many of the non-profit-making organizations like hospitals and educational establishments are still structured in a hierarchical way but there has been a move towards more open communication. Due to the influence of the mass media patients are more knowledgeable and, in general, want to ask questions and discuss their cases. Research has shown that those medical practitioners who encourage two-way flow of communication in consultations tend to have a higher number of satisfied patients (Tuckett *et al.*, 1985).

Some educational establishments have adopted a more democratic form of management, with both staff and students having an input to general policy decisions. There has also been a move towards teaching and learning methods which allow students to be more self-actualizing, to take responsibility for their own learning and to take initiatives in research and project work. This is partly a response to the demands of employers who need a more enterprising and creative workforce. But it is partly also the result of educational research carried out in the 1960s, when most of the methods currently being advocated were first introduced. Many of those in charge of colleges and universities were themselves educated in the 1960s and 1970s and may have been influenced by the theories of that time.

> **Does the culture of an organization in which you are involved reflect any of the values or methods of communication described above? Is it democratic and consultative? Or authoritarian? Are people encouraged to self-actualize? How important are the rules? How many rules are there? Do they seem petty or sensible? Who makes the important decisions and how much say do you have in how the organization operates? Has the organizational culture changed in any way in the time you have been involved in it? Why or why not?**

Organizational Structure

Hierarchies

In analysing organizational cultures we have already referred to one organizational structure – the hierarchy, in which communication flows predominantly downwards through a well-defined chain of command. It may be represented diagrammatically as follows:

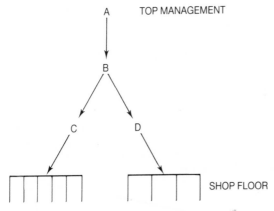

Fig 8.1

At each level in this type of structure there may be individuals who become 'gatekeepers'. These are people who are in a position to pass on information to those under them or to hold back the information. Having information in hierarchical organizations represents a form of power. Those who have access to financial information, for example, will be in a much better position to take decisions on future strategies. Withholding information from people further down the hierarchy may prevent them from being able to take part in important strategic decisions.

Gatekeepers with a high need for power may withhold information partly to maintain the power to take decisions, and partly to prevent bright young people under them from putting forward alternative strategies which might prove more attractive to those further up the hierarchy. If such people were to obtain promotion they might prove a threat to the job, power and authority of the more senior staff member.

Other gatekeepers may not deliberately withhold information, but be so overworked and have so much information to deal with in the course of a day that some of it simply gathers dust in a file and is never passed on. There may be occasions when gatekeepers pass on distorted information – not deliberately, but because they have picked it up wrongly from the person above them. And, of course, gatekeepers can control the information which passes up the line also, making it difficult for those at the bottom to communicate with those at the top.

In organizations where it is difficult for information to flow through the formal channels of communication, informal information systems may take over. In the absence of real information people will speculate about what is going to happen. Snippets of overheard conversations will be exchanged over lunch and rumours may be reported as facts or exaggerated to create fears and tensions about job losses or some other emotive issue. These informal communication channels are often referred to as 'the grapevine'.

Grapevines can have a positive effect. They provide an opportunity for informal communication and the development of relationships between members of an organization. They also serve as a channel whereby new members of the organization can learn about the unwritten rules of behaviour – for example, which boss is likely to appreciate a joke and which one prefers strictly businesslike behaviour; whether it is considered acceptable to go off a few minutes early on a Friday; and what the organization's attitude is towards people who become ill or are struggling to keep up with their work.

The grapevine allows all the stories – good and bad – about the organization's past to be re-told and embellished in a way that demonstrates how present workers feel about the organization and the people in it. It enables staff to pass on information about its culture and values. It may also help develop cohesion among workers, a sense of involvement and identification with the organization and the people in it.

What form does the grapevine take in an organization in

which you are involved? What kind of stories are passed on through the grapevine which reveal the culture, values and attitudes of the organization and the people in it?

Centralization

In hierarchical organizations decisions are taken at the top. In the *centre–periphery structure*, or *centralized system*, the main decisions are taken by a central policy group which usually also comprises top managers. Information is fed out from the central office to other parts of the organization. These other parts may themselves be ordered either hierarchically or in a more democratic way. Within a centralized organization the various peripheral groups may have relatively little contact with each other, and information about important matters thus flows from the centre to the periphery and back without consultation between the peripheral groups. The central office collates the information received from the various groups and takes decisions which are then passed on. This can be shown diagramatically as follows:

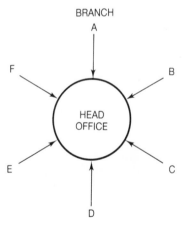

BRANCH
A

F

B

HEAD
OFFICE

E

C

D

Fig 8.2

A good example is the hotel chain. Each hotel is an organization in its own right. Decisions about the day-to-day running of each hotel will be taken by management and staff in the hotel. Decisions which affect the whole chain of hotels will be taken by top managers in the head office. If head office decides to standardize menus, decor, uniforms and the types of services offered, each hotel will have to go along with this decision.

Centralization can be cost-effective. Purchases can be made in bulk and distributed to the various branches. Marketing and advertising can be organized centrally so that the company puts out a consistent image in its publicity material. Standards can be laid down for each branch and those which do not perform adequately can be identified and steps taken to improve their performance. This may involve better staff training, putting in new management or sending someone from central office to do an audit which will identify wasteful or inefficient practices.

Even more important is the ability of the centralized organization to produce a set of logos and other identifying features which will be used on all the company's literature and in the decor of its various branches. This enables customers to recognize the company and provides a method whereby the organization can communicate its corporate image both to those outside and within it.

It isn't only large centralized organizations which try to present a consistent image which will be recognized immediately by those outside the firm. Small self-contained firms may also try to standardize the logos on all their advertising and publicity materials, staff uniforms, premises and company cars as means of differentiating their company from others, telling customers that the company exists, and what business it is in.

> **Take a few minutes to reflect on or discuss the following questions. What is the corporate image of an organization that you are involved in? How is it communicated to those within and outside the organization? Who took the decisions about its image, and how has its particular image evolved? If your organization has no clear corporate image, why is this? Does it affect the operation of the organization? Why or why not?**
>
> **It might make an interesting project to analyse the corporate image of two nation-wide organizations and to produce a visual display which clearly shows either the differences or similarities in their corporate images.**

People who rise to the top in centralized organizations can exercise considerable power and this may satisfy those with strong power needs. For people with high affiliation needs the company which promotes a strong corporate image can produce a satisfying sense of belonging. Many centralized companies have a positive policy of fostering this through communication devices such as company newsletters that contain information about the various branches and the people in them. They are distributed to all the branches and workers are invited to contribute news about hobbies, achievements or points of view. There may also be regular personal letters from the chairman to the workforce, giving information about the company's aims, praise for work done and encouragement to keep up the good work.

Suggestion boxes may be installed within the branches to enable workers to put forward ideas for improvements in company operation. Some companies offer prizes for the best suggestion. Others run competitions for 'employee of the month' or 'best branch'. Winners will have photographs displayed in all the branches and competition to succeed may be keen. This may help satisfy achievement needs and, again, promote identification with the firm. Conferences, centralized training courses and social get-togethers can encourage interaction and communication between people in different departments or branches of the operation.

Those with high achievement needs may find that centralized companies offer more prospects for promotion, since there is not only an opportunity to advance within the branch, but also to move to higher posts in other branches or at headquarters.

People who are self-actualizers may find it more difficult to obtain satisfaction. Centralization may stifle individuality and make it difficult for radically new ideas to be implemented quickly. Workers in low-status roles may find it possible to influence minor policy decisions but more difficult to influence major decisions or to have innovative ideas adopted (Byars, 1984).

Many of the practices outlined above have been borrowed from Japan where there is a strong paternalistic culture. The top manager of an organization is regarded as a father who has parental responsibility to ensure that the family of workers is satisfied. Staff facilities like canteens and rest rooms should be clean and attractive, showing workers that they are valued members of the firm. Care for the social welfare of workers will be expressed in good sickness benefits and the like. Personnel staff will have responsibility for ensuring that workers who have personal worries can discuss these and be given help. This caring attitude may also extend to the spouses and families of workers. (Tung, 1984; Pascale *et al.*, 1981).

In Britain, Marks & Spencer was ahead of its time and adopted a similar approach many years ago. The policy was adopted because the original chairman was convinced that it was the right one. But it was not adopted through altruism. There were sound business reasons for it. A satisfied workforce tends to be a productive workforce, and companies with low industrial unrest tend to attract better staff and be more profitable and successful in the marketplace.

Decentralized Structures

In decentralized structures power is not concentrated in the hands of a few decision-makers. People at all levels will have a chance to influence major policy decisions and to participate in the decision-making process. Power to decide what should be done will be devolved to those who actually have to carry out the work. The role of top management is to achieve *consensus* among the various groups as to what should be done, and, if necessary, to act as final arbitrator if there is a dispute which cannot be resolved democratically. Those at the top can take an overview of the whole organization but will not have absolute power to force their will on others without their consent, except on rare occasions when decisions must be taken quickly and consensus cannot be achieved by discussion or a democratic vote.

There will tend to be opportunities for a free flow of communication throughout the organization, making it easy for people to communicate with others. Diagramatically this could be represented as follows:

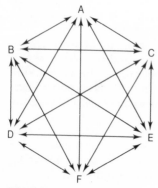

Fig 8.3

One of the problems with free communication flow, democracy and consensus management is that decisions may take longer to be arrived at and those who are in the minority when a democratic vote is taken may feel that they have lost out. On the positive side, it does give a feeling of involvement, responsibility and power. Decisions taken by a democratic process may be adhered to voluntarily because people feel that, even if the decision is one with which they don't agree, they have had a fair chance to put forward their views, and to try to persuade others by arguing the merits of their case.

If consensus management is combined with profit-sharing so that everyone in the organization benefits materially from the company's success, this may prove a winning combination both in terms of worker satisfaction and organizational development (Heller, 1984; Hickman & Silva, 1985; Lessem, 1985a; Waterman, 1988).

Most decentralized organizations produce a statement of the organizational aims known as a *mission statement*. This is circulated to all of those within the organization and is usually incorporated in annual reports or other documents which are sent to shareholders or others outside the organization. The aims are part of the organization's *corporate strategy* for development. This is arrived at by a process of democratic consultation. The aims are translated into long- and short-term objectives and action plans, for which specific individuals or groups will take 'ownership' and responsibility for ensuring that they are achieved (Fawn & Cox, 1987; Deal & Kennedy, 1982; Naisbitt, 1984).

Matrix Structures

Many decentralized organizations now work on matrix management principles (Rowen *et al.*, 1980; Galbraith, 1971). The matrix structure is not based on hierarchical levels but takes the form of a grid, comprising a number of small project teams. Each team has its own leader, and members of the team are drawn from a variety of different disciplines or departments within the organization. Teams are responsible for controlling their own budgets, for setting objectives and carrying them out, for quality control and for their own marketing and promotional strategies.

Some of these project teams will be fairly stable units responsible for long-term work. Others will be set up for a particular short-term purpose. There will be opportunities for people to move between teams, or to disband teams and form new ones as the need arises. In some cases people may work within more than one team – perhaps having a leadership role in one and a membership role in another. There will be opportunities for communication both within and between teams. A typical matrix structure is shown below.

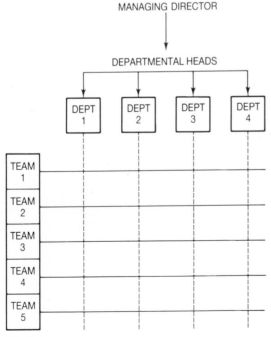

Fig 8.4

The benefits of matrix structures are that devolved power makes them more democratic. They can be more flexible and responsive to change, and workers can move throughout the organization, gaining experience in a range of different areas. The disadvantages are that those within teams may jealously guard their power and try to build up their own little empire without regard for the needs of other teams or the overall good of the organization. Strongly cohesive teams may produce good work but may try to prolong the existence of their team by ensuring that the work continues, even when it is either not cost-effective or not in the general interest of the organization for it to continue.

Creativity, Brainstorming and Quality Circles

With the current emphasis on entrepreneurialism and innovation, organizational managers may perceive a need to foster both creativity and quality within the company in order to achieve success in the marketplace. One method of doing so is to set up 'brainstorming' sessions either within project teams or within groups brought together specifically for the purpose of producing new ideas.

Brainstorming involves generating as many ideas as possible in a very short time. There is no attempt to evaluate the ideas at this stage, and all ideas are written down regardless of how bizarre or stupid they seem. Once all the ideas are collected those which seem feasible are put to one side for later consideration. Those which seem bizarre or downright daft are then considered – not in order to prove how unworkable they are, but rather to see whether by exploring them it is possible to arrive at a novel approach which might not have been so easily achieved if the obviously workable ideas had been considered first. The final stage is comparison of the novel approaches with the more conventional approaches to see whether the novel approaches still offer better possibilities for innovation or problem-solving. Many innovative product lines have been developed in this way – for example, the idea of the transverse engine in the Mini arose out of a brainstorming session to look at possible designs for a new small car. The apparently daft idea of putting the engine in upside down, was the trigger for the suggestion to put it in sideways and led to one of the most successful innovations in car design (De Bono, 1981; Majaro, 1988).

> Cows belch methane from both ends! This is a problem in that it is contributing to the greenhouse effect and damage to the ozone layer. Have a brainstorming session with a group of friends to see if you can come up with an idea for solving this problem!

Another technique for producing new and better ways of doing things is the use of *quality circles*. These are groups which meet together under a group leader who comes prepared with a list of aspects of operation which are causing problems or need to be improved. As a result of brainstorming or general discussion, solutions may be put forward. Actions to be carried out, and the time-scale for them, are decided within the group. Individuals then volunteer, or are asked, to take personal responsibility for ensuring that what has been decided on does happen within the time-scale determined.

If the individuals fail to achieve the desired action in the given time, there will be an opportunity to discuss why at a subsequent meeting and either to extend the deadline or look for a different course of action. There should be no condemnation of someone who fails to achieve. Rather, the approach should be supportive and problem-solving with all of those in the group suggesting ways of moving forward.

The name 'quality circles' arose because the problems which were first tackled in this way arose out of a need to improve product quality, to increase customer satisfaction and cut down on the costs involved in scrapping or replacing faulty goods. It has the added advantage of reducing the need for supervision and quality checks since each production unit is responsible for maintaining the quality of its own work (Bedoyere, 1988).

Moving into the 1990s

Advances in technological methods of communication have now made it possible for people in organizations in America, Japan and Europe to participate in a meeting or conference without leaving their own desks. Satellites, and the use of telephones, videos, computers and fax machines make it possible for people to communicate over great distances as though they were in the same room. Documents can be typed in America or Japan and printed out, almost immediately, on a machine in Britain. People can discuss, make decisions or solve problems without the expenditure of time and energy required to bring them all together in one place. At the moment the technology is relatively expensive. In the future it may be cheap and commonplace (Handy, 1984).

People can also learn at a distance through television or by programmes installed on home computers. The Open University and The Open College provide examples of educational organizations which are not confined to a particular building. This form of organization may become more prevalent in the future.

Facilities already exist for computer shopping and banking without leaving one's home. Rank Xerox has set up an experimental network of business organizations in which people work from their own homes and communicate with others in the network through computers and other technological aids (Judkins *et al.*, 1985).

Electronic mail, transmitted via computers within an organization, can now be used as an alternative to face-to-face communication. This not only speeds up communication but reduces the possibilities for gatekeeping since information sent by computer is difficult to keep secret and the effective use of a computer network means that there has to be open access to information throughout the organization.

Conclusions

Rather than provide a summary of this chapter, or outline what we see as the pros and cons of information and communication technology, we end with a series of questions:

> **What are the various organizational structures and what are their different effects on:**
>
> **communication;**
> **management style;**
> **culture;**
> **values;**
> **organizational success, creativity or growth;**
> **satisfying the needs of the workforce?**
>
> **What are the possible implications for organizational communication if the use of information technology increases markedly?**
> **How might organizational structures be affected?**
> **How might this affect the motivation and satisfaction of employees and managers?**
> **What might be the effects on profitability and productivity?**
> **What are other possible advantages and disadvantages?**
> **What organizational patterns do you envisage in the year 2000, bearing in mind the introduction of the Single European Market legislation in 1992?**

REFERENCES

BEDOYERE, Q. DE LA (1988): *Managing people and problems*. Gower

BLAKE, R. & MOUTON, J. (1964): *The managerial grid*. Gulf

BURNS, T. & STALKER, G.M. (1962): *The management of innovation*. Tavistock

BYARS, L.L. (1984): *Strategic management*. Harper & Row

DEAL, T.E. & KENNEDY, A.A. (1982): *Corporate planning in practice*. Kogan Page

DE BONO, E. (1981): *Atlas of management thinking*. Temple Smith

DRUCKER, P.F. (1974): *Management tasks, responsibilities, practice*. Harper & Row

—— (1985): *Innovation and entrepreneurship*. Heinemann

FAWN, J. & COX, B. (1987): *Corporate planning in practice*. Kogan Page

GALBRAITH, J.R. (1971): Matrix organization designs. *Business Horizons* 14(1), 29–40

HANDY, C. (1984): *The future of work*. Basil Blackwell

—— (1988): *Making managers*. Pitman

HELLER, R. (1984): *The supermanagers*. Truman Talley Books

HERZBERG, F. (1966): *Work and the nature of man*. World Press

HICKMAN, H.R. & SILVA, M.A. (1985): *Creating excellence*. Allen & Unwin

JUDKINS, P. (1985): *Networking in organizations*. Gower

LESSEM, R. (1985a): *Enterprise development*. Gower

—— (1985b): *The roots of excellence*. Fontana/Collins

McGREGOR, D. (1960): *The human side of enterprise*. McGraw-Hill

McLELLAND, D.C. & WINTEER, D.G. (1969): *Motivating economic achievement*. The Free Press

MAJARO, S. (1988): *The creative gap*. Longman

MAYO, E. (1933): *The human problems of an industrial civilisation*. Macmillan

—— (1986): *Re-inventing the corporation*. Macdonald

NAISBITT, J. (1984): *Megatrends*. Warner Books

PASCALE, R. & AMOS, A. (1981): *The art of Japanese management*. Simon & Schuster

PORTER, L.W. & LAWLER, E.E (1968): *Managerial attitudes and performance*. Irwin

RICKARDS, T. (1985): *Stimulating innovation*. Frances Pinter

ROWEN, T.D. (1980): The pros and cons of matrix management. *Administrative Management* 41, 22–4

TUCKETT, D. (1985): *Meetings between experts*. Tavistock

TUNG, B. (1984): *Key to Japanese economic strength: human power*. Lexington

VROOM, V.H. (1967): *Work and motivation*. Wiley

WATERMAN, P.H. (1988): *The renewal factor*. Bantam Press

WATSON, T.T. (1963): *A business and its beliefs*. McGraw-Hill

CHAPTER NINE

THE INTERVIEW

In any organization interviews between individuals are an important aspect of communication. Interviews are often used to decide who will or will not be chosen to become part of an organization. Interviewing brings together many of the components of communication which we have been examining – listening, perception, verbal and non-verbal communication, and, above all, attitudes.

An interview is a situation in which one or more persons is giving or eliciting information from a person or a group. It is usually carried out in a definite time frame and in many cases a formal setting.

Types of interview

There is a wide range of interviews: the selection, appraisal, grievance, disciplinary and counselling. Each has its particular structures and therefore each possesses particular characteristics in terms of the patterns of communication. In this section we will briefly explore the various types to show these characteristics.

Selection Interviews

The aim of this interview is to find the most appropriate person for a particular job from a number of candidates; these have normally been short-listed by a scrutiny of application forms. The setting is usually formal: the interviewee faces his or her questioner, or a panel, across a desk. Initial questions are asked which attempt to break the ice, then there follows a period of intense questioning in which the candidate's previous work experience, qualifications, motivation, interests and ambitions will be probed.

Interviews vary enormously in length but many will take 20 minutes to half an hour to complete. The candidate is given an opportunity to ask questions and the proceedings may well be accompanied by tests of some kind or a tour of the premises.

Think back to any interview that you have had – we're certain that you've had at least one – at school, getting to college, university, applying for a part-time job, permanent employment or a volunteer placement.

Jot down some of the factors which made this particular interview a pleasant or unpleasant experience. You might select one of each if you've had enough experience of being 'grilled'. Reflect on the setting, the kinds of question and the manner in which they were asked.

In selection interviews, the candidate is aiming to make the best possible impression; he or she does this by paying attention to dress, grooming and deportment.

In fact there are numerous books on the market of the 'How to Succeed at your Next Interview' type which aim to provide expert advice to the candidate on these points. This is what Goffman (1958) has called 'Impression Management'; he likens it to an actor playing a role putting on a mask for the performance and then taking it off again when the show is over (see Chapter Six, p.000).

The aim of the interviewers is to see through this 'mask', to probe beneath the surface and to discover the real motives and abilities of the candidate. We should therefore expect to hear a number of questions which attempt to clarify information provided. Such questions as:

Could you I wonder expand a little . . .?
Am I right in thinking that . . .?
Could I ask you to clarify this . . .?

Many of these questions will relate directly to the information that the candidate has supplied on the application form. In fact Goodworth (1985) has suggested that the sole purpose of any selection interview is to 'carry out a comprehensive and accurate background investigation to seek out and verify the facts of past achievement'.

It is true that the application form will usually provide the interview with some kind of structure. This can be described as:

Your PAST – Your PRESENT – Your FUTURE (with us?)

Alternatively the interview may start at the present, the here and now, and then move, as in the structure:

Your PRESENT – How did you get there? Where are you GOING to?

Many interviewers start with one of these structures in mind but find it very difficult to follow. This is especially true when there is a panel of interviewers, since it is then more likely that there will be a confusion of directions, unless that is the panel have worked together and established some internal harmony of approach or have arrived at a clear decision as to who will ask particular questions and in what order.

There are certain dangers with a highly structured approach to any interview and this is very apparent in selection. The interviewer rigidly adhering to a particular structure may miss useful information because it is off the track and outside the orbit of the questioning. On the other hand it is very important to achieve some kind of consistency in the different interviews that may take place during a day or morning. To help achieve this some degree of structuring is necessary so that one can be reasonably sure that the main ground will be covered and that one candidate is not unfairly advantaged or disadvantaged against another.

Many of those carrying out selection interviews appear to have a very generous idea as to their own capabilities to assess candidates within half an hour or so. They believe that in that time it is possible to measure the applicant's intelligence, motivation, ability to solve problems, communication skills and sensitivity to stressful situations. Research into the reliability and validity of the selection interview (Cooper 1981, Schmidt and Stitt 1981) shows that many of these factors are very difficult to assess accurately even where the interview is supplemented by a battery of specialized and well-authenticated tests, administered within a generous allocation of time by those specially trained in such testing.

More and more companies and organizations are now supplementing the selection interview with psychological tests and other devices – even graphology (the study of a person's handwriting for particular clues as to character, etc.). Hand-in-hand with this has come the growing realization that effective selection interviewing demands interpersonal skills of the highest order.

The Appraisal Interview

In some ways this bears a resemblance to the selection interview, in that the setting is usually formal, appraiser and appraisee sit opposite each other, clarification questions are very much to the fore and a form, called a performance review or staff development form, is referred to. However, there are substantial differences which affect the nature of communications between the two.

An appraisal interview is held to review a member of staff's performance over a given period – usually one year – and to enable management and supervisors to agree with that member of staff a programme of development which will serve to correct any faults and/or exploit recognized potential.

In the selection interview there is very little negotiation as to what will occur. It is true that on occasions, particularly in more senior appointments, there may be some attempt by the interviewer to negotiate with the candidate the topics which will be covered, but normally the agenda of the interview is very much the property of the selectors. In appraisal interviews the aim is to reach agreement, a shared understanding between appraiser and appraisee as to (a) what has been covered in the interview, and (b) what will happen as a result of these discussions in terms of career developments, training etc.

Hence one would expect to find in the appraisal interview not only a number of clarification questions as in any selection but also questions relating to negotiation as in:

Would you think that could help you?
How do you personally feel about such a course?
Can we agree that this cannot continue?

As in any negotiation both parties may start the proceedings far apart and then gradually close up. The goal is to reach an agreed statement which both parties can sign. The appraiser must allow the appraisee to take a full part in the proceedings. This means rather more than having the chance to ask a few questions; it implies a deliberate strategy to allow full participation. This may be achieved by the use of open questions:

How do you feel about your present job?

These provide the appraisee with opportunities to enter fully into the discussion. Many companies send out full details of the appraisal to staff so that they will be able to prepare ahead. In some cases self-appraisal forms are issued so that the interview will centre on the individual's concerns and judgements.

The conclusion of any appraisal is crucial in determining its success or failure (Koontz and O'Donnell, 1984). Promises or commitments made during the interview must be checked for mutual understanding. A summary of the main points should be written down and a copy provided for both parties. Commitments entered into must be firmly adhered to.

Grievance and Disciplinary Interviews

The main aim of these interviews is to sort out fact from supposition. A member of staff has a grievance; he or she comes to the manager and lodges a grievance – a complaint. This may be against a colleague (e.g., sexual harassment or discrimination based on race or colour). The manager then has the difficult task of discovering the truth.

To do this there will have to be a process of clarification; in some ways there is a resemblance to a law court:

When did it happen?
Was there anyone else present.
Has this re-occurred?

The manager's role, apart from asking the questions, is to be a keen and disinterested listener – he or she cannot afford to take sides or pre-judge the issue until all the facts have been gathered.

The disciplinary interview occurs when a manager is not satisfied with the performance, conduct or attitude of a member of staff and decides the time has come for immediate action. Most organizations have precise written codes to guide the management and staff. By following these much of the sting can be taken out of any confrontation (Maude, 1982).

The interviewer, however, must make absolutely certain that the main facts of the situation are communicated clearly to the interviewee. Ambiguity at this stage will lead to trouble in later proceedings, especially if matters reach an Industrial Tribunal.

The atmosphere and layout of the interview is usually formal; this indicates to the interviewee that 'this is no easy chat'. However, the danger with that formula is that the interview becomes a frightening and generally disagreeable experience.

> **Think back to any 'interview' that you have experienced where you were disciplined for some reason – fairly or unfairly. What were your reactions to this?**

Most likely you came out of the interview feeling annoyed or even aggressive. Training in Transactional Analysis (see page 000) can be of great help to managers in these situations since it provides a means for analysing the 'transactions' that take place over the desk and enables managers to appreciate how certain strategies can reduce the risk of annoyance and even aggression.

It is vital that there should be in any disciplinary interview some measure of consistency in the handling of such interviews between departments, plants and sections of an organization. If this sort of conversation ensues in the staff room then one can be pretty certain that there is no overall consistent approach to the handling of disciplinary issues:

A: My manager called me into his office and gave me a friendly warning about my coming in late.

B: Well, that's funny, I was given a written warning for the same thing a couple of months ago and I was told it was my last one.

That's the kind of inconsistency which will soon undermine trust in any system of discipline within an organization.

Market Survey Interviews

We can define this as a situation where the interviewer attempts to get as much information as possible from the interviewee in as short a time as possible.

> **Have you ever been stopped in the street and your opinion**

asked for on an aspect of what you buy in the shops, what party you might vote for, cause your support, newspapers you read or TV programmes you regularly watch? If you can answer yes to any of these, then you have been involved in a market survey interview.

What were your feelings?

How did you react?

These interviews will be very carefully structured so as to ensure consistency. This is obviously very important where one has a number of interviewers spread around the country all attempting to discover very much the same information. There is therefore a high degree of supervision of the results from each 'collector', together with the use of sophisticated computer sampling which aims to show up freak results, an indication of possible faulty interviewing.

In such interviews we would expect questions which have been designed for such computer analysis. For example:

Q: How many hours per day do you normally watch TV?

A: None . . . 2 hours . . . 4 . . . 6 . . . more than 6 hours.

Q: Of these hours approximately how much do you spend watching ITV?

A: None . . . 2 hours . . . 4 . . . 6 . . . more than 6 hours.

The interviewer ticks or circles the appropriate box. There is no time here for supplementary questions or amplifications that are not written into the list of questions. The interviewer's job then is to move the interviewee rapidly but carefully through the list and to gain as much information as possible. All this has to be done in the middle of a busy shopping arcade, street, railway station or airport surrounded by noise and bustle. Some interviews take place in people's homes. These are normally pre-arranged and can therefore be a little more relaxed.

The Interview as Communication

We have listed the various types of interview and commented briefly on their particular structures. We now turn to investigate the elements of communication that are common.

Non-verbal Communication in the Interview

If you are working with a group you might like to try out this little experiment. Simulate as far as possible the conditions for an interview. Role play the part of the candidate and the interviewer(s). The candidate(s) should 'play' different types with very different non-verbal communication to match. For example, the very positive type with confident posture, head

held high, firm handshake, etc. Then the less confident one
with little eye contact, less firm handshake, etc.

The aim is to see what effect these variations in performance have in terms of your rating of the candidates. Take
them through the first few minutes of the interview.

If you're using this book on your own, you might like to
consider carefully your feelings when you encounter someone in a social setting for the first time. How are your feelings for that person influenced by the non-verbal factors he
or she exhibited at the opening of the encounter?

There is a good deal of evidence from research (Ley, 1976) that first
impressions gathered at the start of an interview can be quite hard
to shift. What tends to happen is that a good first impression may
be reinforced by subsequent performance rather than a weak first
impression being redeemed.

We noted in Chapter Three on non-verbal communication that eye
contact is a very powerful channel of communication. There is a
measure of agreement that a lack of such contact between candidate
and interviewer at the start of an interview will create poor first
impressions (Argyle, 1982).

When a candidate is faced with a panel of interviewers, it is
necessary that he or she should establish eye contact with each
person on the panel while at the same time addressing the person
asking the question.

An interesting study was done by Imada and Hakel (1977) in which
they tested interviewers' responses to candidates who emitted
positive non-verbal clues, defined as 'high degree of eye contact, alert
posture, firm handshake', as opposed to those who emitted a
negative series of clues – low eye contact, slouching posture and limp
handshake or none at all. They found that interviewers responded
much more favourably to the 'positive' candidates, rating them
twice as likely for recommendation to hire and three times as likely to
succeed. Interestingly enough the study also found that even where
qualifications were evenly matched between the two groups, the
'positive' candidates' qualifications were much better thought of,
i.e., 'your degree is better because I respond more to you and the
positive signals you emit'.

Paying Attention and Listening in the Interview

We have examined the nature of listening in Chapter Four. The interview provides a demanding test of the ability to listen for both interviewer and interviewee. Where we are meeting people for the first
time, as in a selection interview, our attitudes may well be triggered
by a host of different, even minute, factors.

The 'halo effect', which we met in Chapter Two, is a manifestation of how attitudes can affect the way in which we selectively listen and pay attention to some factors during an interview while at the same time conveniently ignoring others. This effect is illustrated where one factor in the candidate appeals very strongly to the interviewer – 'he's a mountain climber, so he's tough, a useful leader, keen and determined'. This one factor can cause a 'halo' to appear over his candidature, thus helping to minimize any deficiencies. The negative halo effect works in exactly the opposite way: a negative impression being caused by one apparent deficiency.

It's as though a veil is drawn down and reality slightly distorted. This effect may influence our subsequent listening: we may well home-in on those parts of the conversation that reinforce the impression that we have already made.

We saw how the slow speaker is often perceived as being less incisive and dynamic than the one who speaks fluently and uses more variety of stress and inflexion. If during the interview, especially at the start, the candidate does speak slowly – hesitantly, it is all too easy to make the correlation that such a person is indecisive – lacking in dynamism. We know that much of this hesitancy is due to nerves.

There are a number of other ways in which our attitudes may affect the manner to which we attend and listen to an interview. Before reading further do please refer back to our section on listening in Chapter Four.

Look at this extract from a selection interview:

Interviewer: Would you go over for me your experience as a manager with your last firm?

Candidate: I found it challenging, I must say.

How might the interviewer who had already formed a negative impression of this candidate 'listen' to that reply, remembering that we tend to 'listen with our brains not just our ears'?

Interviewer: (*Thinks: 'Challenge, I bet it was. Couldn't cope.'*)

And then a few minutes later into the interview:

Interviewer: Did you find this particular assignment stimulating?

Candidate: Yes, very much so. Luckily I had a very good team to assist me.

Interviewer: (*Thinks: 'Leant on them all the time, I'm sure!'*)

Could you construct a short dialogue on these lines where instead of a *negative* halo effect, as in the above, there is a *positive* one? Underneath the actual words spoken put down the thoughts of the interviewer.

In many interviews – selection in particular – there are certain other problems that may affect how listening is carried out. There is, for instance, the problem of fatigue. Attempting to interview a number of candidates in one morning presents the interviewer(s) with the very real danger of fatigue and loss of concentration. Pity the poor candidate who arrives before the lunch break. But then again he or she might be given some attention because at least a break in the proceedings is at hand. Perhaps our real sympathies should lie with the penultimate candidate.

There is also the difficulty when one candidate who is very fluent and self-confident is immediately followed by one who is rather quiet and nervous. The effect of such a contrast may well be to damage the second one out of all proportion to his or her actual abilities. The effects of this kind of normative comparision can be reduced if the criteria for the post are carefully worked through: judgement is then more clearly focused on whether that candidate can achieve the demands of the post rather than how he or she compares with other candidates.

We saw in the chapter on listening, page 57, that negative feelings towards the speaker may then affect the way in which we select, distort and filter incoming signals. These feelings also have a reciprocating effect, i.e., the speaker may detect that we are not really listening and this may affect his or her performance.

Consider this example. An unemployed person comes for an interview with a counsellor. She is rather nervous about coming and made more so by the apparent attitude of the counsellor who appears not really to be listening to her problems. This further reduces her confidence, she says less; this in turn convinces the counsellor that she isn't that serious about wanting to find work. We have then a viscious circle, a self-fulfiling event in which the quality of communication suffers.

Reflection

Reflection as a listening technique was discussed in Chapter Four, page 60. In many training courses for interviewers time is spent on developing the technique of reflection. The following short extract from an interview shows how it may be employed in practice.

We eavesdrop to part of a social worker's busy day. She is interviewing an elderly person who, because of ill health, has had to give up her home to live in in sheltered housing.

Social worker: How are you settling in Mrs Dixon?
Client: Fine, but it takes some getting used to, not having your own place.
Social worker: It's quite a change from home?
Client: It's being here, all these other people around all the time, the noise, the coming and going.

Social worker:	You haven't really got used to it?
Client:	I do miss having the neighbours around, you see. It seems so strange not having them popping in.
Social worker:	You'll find it a bit on the lonely side.
Client:	I expect I'll make new friends; it takes time. They're all very nice here I must say.
Social worker:	I'm sure you'll make new friends, no trouble. Now let me just ask. . . .

Notice how the social worker is responding to her client. She is not trying at this stage to pump her for information, that would be unsettling and counter-productive. She is trying to reflect her client's feelings, apprehensions, misgivings, back to her.

This process of reflection can achieve several ends: it helps reassure the interviewee that the social worker, interviewer, is actually paying attention. Secondly, in some cases merely having the situation or problem 'bounced' back helps reduce it in scale and immediacy.

Try this out for yourself. Be careful to reflect accurately the other person's feelings. Don't be tempted to add your own ideas – that's not reflection.

One person, for instance, has a problem and has come for some assistance. Take it in turns to be the reflector. If you have a cassette recorder handy it would be worthwhile recording the piece, playing it back and analysing it.

Questions in the Interview

You might suppose that all questions are the same; well you'd be quite wrong. We have already mentioned open questions in our section on market survey interviews. There are a number of others.

Open questions are used to elicit a response where what is wanted is a completely free, unrestricted answer.

How do you feel about . . .?
Give me your thoughts on . . .?

These can be of great value for any interview. However, if too many are used too often the interviewer, unless care is taken over recording and subsequent classification, may be swamped with data. Also if the interviewer is making use of computer-based retrieval systems then such questions will have to be thought through very carefully because computers do not normally appreciate having to deal with such wide-ranging responses.

The closed question limits the respondant to yes/no replies:

Did you complete the course?
Did you watch any ITV programmes last night?

The closed question can be very useful in getting to the heart of the matter quickly. There then might follow some open questions for elaboration.

We could represent this diagramatically as:

_____ Closed _____

_____ Open

However, we might reverse this and start with a number of wide-ranging open questions, then home-in on a number of points raised before opening up again:

_____ Closed _____

Open _____ Open

A thorough interview would resemble much more of a mixture of open and closed questions; the closed used to verify and harden up on points raised. Hence:

_____ Closed __   _____ Closed __   _____ Closed __

Open _____ Open _____ Open _____

In hardening up on information supplied use may be made of the *clarification* question. We have already met with this in the appraisal interview. For example,

> Could I ask you to clarify . . .?
> Have I understood you right . . .?

Rather more specialized question types are the *agreement* and *objection* varieties which are extensively used in sales and marketing. Both try and 'lead' the prospective client into a sale. Here is an example of a series of agreement questions:

Sales assistant: Now you're looking for a machine that'll do the job faster, aren't you?
Client: Yes, that's what I want.
Sales assistant: You also said you wanted something rather more reliable . . .?
Client: Er . . . yes.

You can see from this how the ground has been prepared for the close. The sales assistant then says: 'Well, I've got just the thing for you here'.

The objection type question follows a similar pattern. Here again we are listening to a sales assistant in hot pursuit:

Sales assistant: You feel this might be awkward?
or: You're not sure that it matches?
or: You don't want to risk . . .?

You can see how the use of such questions helps to ward off problems and 'steers' the prospect towards the sale.

Language Barriers in the Interview

During all kinds of interviews communication is often hindered by misunderstandings which arise out of words and their meanings. It is generally believed that the problems of jargon (specialized words used in a specialized sense, e.g., medical words) relate to the confusions between specialist and layperson. Some recent research (Tucker, 1984) which focused on doctor–patient communication suggests that the problem may lie in another direction. It is not, suggests Tucker, the fact the the layperson does not know the word – for instance, arthritis – it is much more likely to be that the meaning of that word has different meanings in the mind of the doctor and that of the patient.

We could depict this using a model based on the semiotic perspective which we examined in Chapter Five.

1. <u>   A   </u>   <u>   B   </u>

Here we see how the 'worlds of meaning' possessed by A and B are separate. For instance, there is no sharing of understanding of the word 'arthritis' – it is completely unknown to B. This can easily happen to us when we are faced with legal language or when we go to a garage to find out what has happened to our car which juddered to a halt in a pool of oil.

2. <u>   A   </u><u>   B   </u>

In this second example there is some overlap in understanding between A and B. The word 'arthritis' is known to both of them but, as Tucker suggests, they may well have rather different interpretations of that word. This can give rise to all kinds of difficulties. The doctor using the word and seeing that the patient nods may take it to mean that there is a sharing of meaning. The patient hearing it from the doctor may well assume that he knows what aspect of arthritis is being mentioned. This is where the danger lies: both persons are under the impression that the other knows each other's meaning.

3. <u>   A   </u>
    <u>   B   </u>

In the third case we see how there is a complete overlap of understanding; perhaps in this situation the doctor is talking with a colleague: they have both studied the disease and both have the same 'mental map' of the subject. There is little likelihood of this happening. Because of the many differences there are bound to be between even two medical colleagues – their clinical experience for one – there will be slight but probably significant connotations built round the single word 'arthritis'. Therefore the perfect overlap of meaning, as illustrated in the third of our models, will depict the ideal rather than the normal.

Apart from jargon itself there are other problems associated with language which may well interfere with the processes of the interview. Look at this example of where one person's understanding of a word is not shared by his interviewer:

Interviewer: How would you describe your management style?
Interviewee: Well, I try to be assertive in the sense that they realize who has to carry the responsibility.
Interviewer: (Not understanding the difference between assertive and aggressive, thinks to himself: *Oh, a bossy type eh? Well, no thanks.*) Yes well, I'm sure that approach is necessary from time to time.

So the interview continues with the applicant dammned as an authoritarian type who will probably inflict untold damage on the staff.

We have used the terms 'steer' and 'lead' a number of times in this section. In many texts on interviewing you will come across the phrase 'leading question'. This is usually defined as a question which directs the interviewee towards the answer. It is dangerous in that if this happens the interviewer will not be in a position to elicit the true feelings, thoughts, ideas and opinions of the subject.

Surely you don't . . .?
You're quite happy aren't you . . .?

These are leading questions in the sense that those being addressed don't have to be very alert or very clever to 'see' where the question is leading. Normally in an interview one is trying to impress, there is thus a temptation to agree with the interviewer, to play along with his or her ideas. Therefore if we can detect where the question is leading we can supply the appropriate answer – not one which we necessarily believe.

There appears to us to be a much deeper problem: ordinary questions which do not appear to be leading may well take on this characteristic if the situation – the context of the interview – is fully appreciated. If a teacher asks a pupil:

Are you enjoying the class?

We could say that this appears to be a very innocent open question. However, if we consider it from the pupil's point of view it might not seem that innocent. Suppose that the pupil is looking for a reference from that teacher. Is this to him not a form of leading question – some kind of test of loyalty? Would he answer in most polite tones:

> Well since you ask, I'm a little disappointed really.

It is therefore vital for any interviewer to consider the likely impact of any questions from the interviewer's point of view. Do they seem threatening? Is there an element of loyalty testing to them? The more the power differential between interviewer and interviewee, the more likely it is that questions will 'lead' or 'pull' towards the expected and 'correct' answer.

Interviewing is all about the elicitation of accurate information; it is not to do with having our own prejudices and opinions faithfully repeated back to us.

Acknowledgement of Interviewee

When we enter into an interview with someone we do not come as a person with no feelings, hopes, complaints, diagnoses or frustrations. We come full of these. If our feelings are not attended to there is every likelihood that we will not pay much attention to the interviewer as we should.

One of the most important aspects of interviewing is to respect the feelings that the interviewee will bring into the room, to open these up, to acknowledge them in a friendly way.

Examine this short extract from an interview between a personnel officer in a company and a member of staff who has been made redundant. Jot down your thoughts as to how far this process of acknowledgement has been taken.

Interviewer: Come in Mrs Smith. It's good to see you. You know why we're having this meeting?

Interviewee: Yes so that I can find a job, but . . .

Interviewer: Yes that's it. Now I see from your record that you've had quite a lot of experience in sales. Have you seen today's paper?

Interviewee: No.

Interviewer: Well there are a good number of jobs in sales. I would have thought that with your experience and with some good references from your department head you would have little problem in finding something. It was full time you were looking for?

Interviewee: Yes, but well. . . .

Interviewer: Yes, I know what you're going to say. You've

Interviewer: been here 10 years and it's going to be very difficult to get used to a whole new set of folk. Well, let me tell you that within a couple of days – a week at most – you'll be wondering whether you actually ever worked here at all.

Interviewee: I'm sure of that.

Interviewer: Now I'd like you to go and see a friend of mine who's very much into sales. Do you know Pinkington's?

Interviewee: Vaguely.

Interviewer: Well they're very much into sales and my friend is the sales director. He'd be able to tell you which companies in the area are or will be looking for staff.

Interviewee: I'm really not sure. You see, I've got this notion of going to college.

Interviewer: No problem. Most employers will be happy to help you with part-time study for your Institute of Marketing Exams – you don't have that, do you?

Interviewee: No.

Interviewer: Well, I would rest easy on that score. There's a college not very far from here which runs these courses. It's a very worthwhile qualification.

Interviewee: I'm not sure I'd want to study for that.

Interviewer: Well, you can think about that once you get the job.

Interviewee: I mean I'm not certain I do want a job.

Interviewer: Pardon?

Interviewee: You see I did have this rather silly notion of going to college and taking some courses to get me into university. But after what you've said I'm not sure now. . . .

No wonder she's not sure. She came into that room with an agenda. She had something she thought was important to say and that something was ignored. Imagine how she must feel towards the interviewer. Is she going to listen with rapt attention to his suggestions until he has negotiated a little more and shared a little further?

Training in Interviewing Skills

Successful interviewing can be seen as more than the possession of a number of separate communication and procedural skills. There is little point in being able to recognize the difference between open and closed questions unless one has some idea of when and how to use them. There has been criticism of the kind of training that may lead to the development of such skills with little or no appreciation of the context in which they may be applied (Pendleton, 1984). A great deal of training in interview skills makes use of the social skills training approach (Argyle, 1982).

This usually follows several distinct stages. First, the student is made aware of the various skills and their dimensions. This is done either by watching a skilled performer or a video of such. Secondly, the student practises the skill; it may be that this is broken down into a series of sub-skills so that practice is made easier (think of driving lessons, each one devoted to a particular aspect or sub-skill of driving). Feedback is provided – again often in video form – and further practice is encouraged. This cycle of feedback, performance, practice, feedback, etc., is continued until the skill itself is grasped. The idea is that feedback will enable the learner to find a pathway to improved performance.

There are, however, a number of criticisms of the SST approach. There is some doubt whether the technique does provide enough understanding of the processes behind the skills (MacIntyre, 1984). MacIntyre suggests that more is needed than just the mastery of a set of skills; an attitude change is often required before the training can become effective. For instance, it is no good training an interviewer to use improved eye contact with the interviewees if that interviewer's attitude towards the person sitting on the other side of the table is one which is negative, or one which stereotypes the candidate before he or she has had a chance to speak.

This leads us to the thorny issue of competence in communication, which we discussed in our Introduction to this book. Hymes (1972) said of this that

> A person's competence in communication should refer to the ability to perform as well as the knowledge of how to perform.

According to this view, then, the interviewer should possess some understanding of the factors that lie behind interpersonal communication. These could include attitude formation and the effect of attitudes on the 'sender' and the 'receiver', plus some knowledge of the need for negotiation of meaning, an awareness of TA and an appreciation of how role behaviour changes under different circumstances. Armed with this kind of theoretical perspective the development of skills becomes a more meaningful process and the skills themselves can be applied in a more appropriate and flexible way.

Conclusion

We have surveyed this wide and complex field and touched in rather more depth on some key issues relating to communication. Interviewing is often a vastly under-rated pastime: anyone can do it given a little practice – that's the general idea.

It is now the fact that in many organizations, public and private, there is disquiet at the state of the 'art'. It is being realized that training in interviewing is needed; that evaluation of such training has to be encouraged and that alternatives to interviewing should be explored.

When we consider just how important interviews are in terms of getting employment, maintaining it and getting satisfaction from it; of how interviews affect our health and welfare and often the education and development of family members, then we should regard it as a very important task which deserves recognition for what it is: interpersonal competence at a very high level.

Summary

1 There are many different varieties of interviewing: selection, appraisal, disciplinary, grievance, counselling and market survey. They have a number factors in common. These range from the ability to ask a variety of different kinds of questions to adopting appropriate non-verbal behaviours.

2 Evidence suggests that first impressions count for a great deal at interviews. This is crucial in selection interviewing but it may, through the operation of the positive and negative halo effects, produce distortions in evaluation.

3 Reflection is a very useful skill to enable the interviewer to assure the interviewee that he or she is actually being listened to. It may also have the benefit of helping the interviewee see problems in a different light.

4 There are a number of different question types that may be used in an interview: these range from the closed and open to the clarification. Leading questions should be avoided. However, most questions can appear to be leading to the interviewee if the relationship between interviewer and interviewee is based on power and influence.

5 When interviewing it is very important to be clear as to terms used, jargon employed, etc.

6 It is crucial for the interviewer to acknowledge the interviewee in terms of his or her wishes, apprehensions and needs. Failure to do so may ruin any likelihood of a rapport being achieved.

7 Training in interview skills is now common. Social skills training which makes use of video to provide feedback on performance is often employed. Critics of this method point to the apparent lack of attention given to understanding of processes as against skills enhancement.

REFERENCES

ARGYLE, M. (1982): *The psychology of interpersonal behaviour.* Penguin

COOPER, W.H. (1981): Ubiquitous halo. *Psychological Bulletin* 90, 218–44

GOFFMAN, E. (1958): *Presentation of self in everyday life.* Penguin

GOODWORTH, C.T. (1985): *Effective interviewing.* Bus Books

HYMES D. (1972): On communicative competence. In Pride, J. & Holmes, J. (eds), *Sociolinguistics.* Penguin

IMADA, A.S. & HAKEL, M.D. (1977): Influence of non-verbal communication and rater proximity on impressions in interviews. *Journal of Abnormal and Social Psychology* 62, 295–300

KOONTZ, H. & O'DONNELL C. (1984): *Management.* McGraw-Hill

LEY, P. (1976): *Communicating with patients.* Croom Helm

McINTYRE, D. (1984): Social skills and teacher training. In Ellis, R. & Whittington, D. (eds), *New directions in social skill training.* Croom Helm

MAUDE, M. (1982): *The grapevine.* Video Arts

PENDLETON, D. (1984): *Social skills: a paradigm of applied social psychology research.* Plenum Press

SCHMIDT, S. & STITT, C. (1981): Why do I like thee? *Journal of Applied Psychology* 66, 324–8

TUCKER, P. (1984): The real problem of doctor–patient jargon. Interview on *Medicine Now*, BBC Radio 4, November 1984

CHAPTER TEN
PRESENTATION AND PERSUASION

We have already discussed some aspects of presentation in Chapter Nine when we noted how self presentation or impression management is an important element in interviewing. In our final chapter we examine presentation skills and in so doing draw together many ideas from earlier sections, especially those relating to verbal and non-verbal communications, together with listening skills.

In doing this we point forward to the topic of mass communication through a brief examination of persuasion. This merits a book to itself; all we can do in a single chapter is to survey a number of key areas and suggest follow-up reading for those interested. In earlier chapters we have examined examples of verbal communication especially in interpersonal settings. Now we extend our investigations to look at what happens when one person speaks to many – an audience.

> **Consider any talk, lecture or presentation that you have heard recently and which you felt involved and interested you. What was the speaker doing that kept your interest? Conversely, consider any such presentation where you felt like falling asleep or leaving the room. Why was this? What was the speaker doing that made you feel this way?**

We expect you have listed a number of features. It will be interesting to compare your rankings with what research into presentation suggests are the criteria for success.

Presentation

Norton (1984), in his investigation into aspects of communicator style, suggests that the ineffective presenter often lacks liveliness especially when it comes to vocal dynamics. These may be defined as relating to variety of tone, pitch and pace of speech.

Norton who was particularly interested in the effectiveness of teachers presenting information in classes to pupils, suggested that in order first to attract and then maintain the listener's attention the teacher should aim to be 'active stylistically', that is he or she should aim to provide stimulus for the audience in terms of facial expression, body movement, gesture, use of space, etc.; and secondly, be 'sender orientated' – keep eye contact with the audience.

Rosenshine (1970) examined factors that stimulated students during lectures so that their attention was gained and held. He concluded that changes in auditory and visual stimuli were important. He placed particular emphasis on the lecturer being able to vary vocal tempo, stress and inflexional patterns. These variations in stimuli were most effective when placed alongside what he termed, 'warm, systematic and businesslike behaviours'.

Message Ordering and its Effect on the Listeners

Brown (1982), who we have already come across in Chapter Four on listening, has investigated the criteria that 'effective' lecturers use when addressing students. Apart from the factors that we have already listed, he believes from his research that the way in which any presentation is structured can make a fundamental difference to the manner in which it is listened to and 'accepted'.

Brown suggests that the speaker would do well to structure his or her material in terms of sequence, or chronology (1950s, 1960s and 1980s); or in terms of spatial distribution (in South Wales as against central Scotland); or as in debates, with the pros and cons of an argument clearly laid out.

Apart from this work as to how lectures are listened to, there has been a considerable amount of research into the actual effect of structure of a message and audience reception. Advertisers in particular have been sponsors of much of this effort.

The Structuring of Written Communication

We will begin by focusing on the way in which the structure of written language – the words, sentences, paragraphs and whole texts – provides us with clues for recognition and interpretation.

If we examine the following:

> We ls hm us ic won d erf ulis

We may puzzle for a moment and then discover that we can make

> Welsh music wonderful is.

Now we have the words but we do not have the correct order. Our knowledge of the language allows us to construct meanings from this string of words. How this 'knowledge' is arrived at is a very controversial area. Some theories suggest that there is an in-built human capacity for encoding and decoding grammar (Chomsky, 1957). Whatever system we use we can perform a substitution and arrive at:

Welsh music is wonderful.

There is evidence (De Sotto, 1960) that Westerners have a characteristic way of interpreting messages based on linear progression – left to right. It seems as though we scan along lines of print looking for clues all the time making estimations as to what might come next. Hence a phrase such as:

In summer it's lovely to be down. . . .

will generate a number of possible endings. Studies as to how we actually process text (Reid, 1982) suggest that a great deal of estimation and prediction goes on as we scan the lines. We look at a phrase and then very often guess the next part. We can do this because we have assimilated so many structures of language that we can make a pretty accurate stab as to what will follow. For instance here:

	beside the seaside
In summer it's lovely to be down	on the beach
	at the sea

Of course, it is quite possible that other endings could be included. It might be that we are reading science fiction and so our sentence ends with:

In summer it's lovely to be down near the Martian ice cap.

This would be an unusual variant and one deliberately written to make us stop and think.

As we scan along lines of print we are then looking for certain clues which will assist us in making sense of the text. One of the devices that writers use is the placing of markers, words such as 'however', 'after', 'next' and 'finally'. These indicate the structure and serve as signposts as to what will follow. Niles (1963) drew attention to this fact. Examine these examples:

We went to the laboratory to see . . . first we . . . then we . . . , finally we. . . .

The words circled present an idea of sequence, in this case a chronological thread running through the sentence. Compare it with the following:

Because we went to the laboratory . . . we were therefore able to. . . .

Here we have a cause and effect structure: when we see the word 'because' at the start of a sentence we can pretty well be sure to meet a consequence to that idea in the second half of the sentence.

In our visit to the laboratory most of us enjoyed . . . a few found . . . but only one of us. . . .

In this sentence the idea of preference is expressed.

Cohesion

When we analyse the structure of written text we need to pay attention to devices which bind the various sentences and phrases together. This binding process is known as cohesion. Look at this passage:

> The sun shone brightly; it had been a perfect afternoon. The winning team passed the podium, the cup gleaming in the captain's hands. The heat from the stadium was overpowering as the presentation was concluded. The Queen left the podium having shaken hands with each member of this great team. The cup was raised aloft to the cheers of the thousands who had packed the stands. No one would ever forget this moment, this triumph, this spendid summer victory.

If we examine this text carefully we can see how the various bits (circled) cohere, or stick, together. 'Sun' (line 1) relates to 'gleaming' (line 2) to 'heat' in the stands (line 3) and finally to 'splendid summer' on the last line.

Likewise, 'winning' (line 1) relates to 'cup' (line 2) and 'presentation' (line 3), to 'Queen ... shaken hands' (line 4), to 'cheers of thousands' (line 5) and finally to 'triumph' and 'victory' on the last line.

> **Try to re-write the above passage in such a way that there is much less cohesion between the various parts. You will find that such a text is a lot more difficult – even annoying – to read.**
>
> **Consider any 'texts' that you have written – essays, projects, etc. Are they easy to follow in terms of cohesion?**

There are very many other factors which will influence us in our reading of any text. We could list our motivation to read, the size of print, quality of paper, paragraphing, use of illustrations, examples, as well as the topicality, depth of research, use of humour, etc. However, the provision of a structure, a pathway and the cohesion of various elements together in a logical pattern will also greatly influence our reader.

Structuring Oral Communication

When it comes to spoken texts we move into a whole new set of problems as regards message organization and interpretation. Unlike the written form, with speech there is no opportunity, unless we record it, to search back and forth along the text. The spoken word is here and gone and often soon forgotten. But from a variety of directions – advertising and political broadcasting in particular – has come a need to discover which possible combinations, organizations and structures of spoken language will convey a message most effectively to a particular audience.

Audience

In any communication consideration must be given to one's audience. This is true in written communication where aspects to do with technical terminology, jargon and sentence complexity need careful scrutiny to try to match them to the needs of the readership. In oral communication it is perhaps even more vital to think about what likely audience will be listening to the presentation. One of the first considerations must be the formality or informality of the occasion. This will affect choice of vocabulary, structures of language and general tone of presentation. Compare the following:

> Good evening folks. It's great to be back here, nothing seems to have changed, especially the warmth of your welcome. I'd like to spend a few minutes just introducing. . . .

> Good evening ladies and gentlemen. It is a great pleasure to be invited to address you this evening. I propose to centre my lecture around three main themes. I shall show how each of these cohere together and in my conclusion I shall attempt to predict. . . .

We can see that these two extracts have very different tones or registers: one is informal, perhaps an address to a lunch club, the other is a lecture to a formal gathering at some institution perhaps. What are some of the distinguishing features? We could list these as:

> *Lexical* – the actual words used. 'Folks' rather than 'ladies and gentlemen'.
> *Use of short forms* – 'I'd' rather than 'I would'.
> *Grammatical structures* – 'I propose to' rather than 'I'd like to'.

We could also examine the length of the texts, the complexity of the contents, the uses of humour, illustration and metaphor. All these would give us information as to the kind of discourse to which we were listening.

There is now a growing literature on the subject of discourse analysis. This includes such questions as: what is a sermon, or a lecture, or a disc jockey's announcement? How do we recognize these as being different? We indicate further reading for you at the end of the chapter if this section has proved interesting.

Primacy and Recency

We have already noted in Chapter Four on listening the influence of memory span on the way we listen and pay attention. Advertisers and the makers of political messages have been interested to discover which, if any, bits of a message are the best or least well attended to. You can see why there should be this kind of interest. If large sums of money are to be spent on a message to the public then it is of more than passing interest to find out where one should place the punch line, the vital fact.

Early research (Lund, 1929) suggested that primacy effects – in other words the beginnings of messages – were the most attended to and remembered. However, Lund's study and many other subsequent ones took place in classrooms where one might expect students to have a tendency to expect that the first part of a message delivered by a teacher figure – the researcher in this case – might have some importance, i.e.: 'now class, listen. . . .'

More recent studies have examined the order effects of different types of messages and their effects on the listener. For instance, in a deductive argument where the thesis is stated first and the proofs follow, it is likely that primacy effects will be strong. For example:

> Sugar is the main cause of dental caries. This can be proved by the fact that . . . and. . . . Furthermore . . . and finally. . . .

In the inductive style of argument the proofs lead into the conclusion or thesis. For example,

> In Western countries more and more sugar is. . . . There is increased consumption of . . . the incidence of dental caries. . . . Therefore it can be said that sugar is the main cause of dental caries.

It is likely, therefore, that in this case recency effects – the ending of the message – will be stronger because this will be freshest in the mind of the listener.

Further studies into primacy/recency effects have concentrated on some of the many variables that may affect the assimilation of a message. These include: involvement of the listener, his or her commitment to the speaker, the strength of the message, its duration and repetition. As far as reinforcement is concerned, it is known that listeners will accept most readily those aspects of a message which 'strike a chord' with their existing attitudes and preferences (Mortensen, 1972). This suggests that, no matter what the ordering is, if there are parts of a message which reinforce existing predispositions in the mind of the listener, then it will be those parts, whether they come at the start, middle or end which will be taken most notice of and possibly remembered.

> **Try this exercise. Give someone a message. Structure it so that it has a definite start, middle and end. Don't allow this person to take any notes as you give the message. Then test for recall. See whether there is a primacy or recency effect.**

Credibility of Presenter

This leads us into the whole issue of presenter credibility. Mortensen (1972) has defined credibility as a 'loose assortment of factors which, when taken together, makes up for a credible performance.' Amongst this loose assortment, research indicates that dynamism is important to a credible presenter. We return here to the criteria put forward earlier by Norton and by Rosenshine. If we consider some of the so-called credible presenters, people such as Martin Luther King, J.F. Kennedy and Billy Graham, they all have one thing very much in common – a certain dynamic quality, an enthusiasm and a zest which infects their audience.

The famous, or infamous, 'Dr Fox' studies (Naftulin & Ware *et al.*, 1973) demonstrated that enthusiasm and expressiveness of an instructor can significantly influence the ratings given by his audience – despite the fact that the audience does not fully understand what he is talking about. The 'Dr Fox' was in fact a trained actor who had been coached to make a presentation to a group of doctors at a medical conference. He was extensively trained in the conventional way of lecturing from a prepared script. He was introduced as 'An expert in Mathematical Gaming Technique'. He spoke fluently but with plenty of eye contact with his audience. He gave numerous examples and quoted extensively from the 'literature', even referring to his own research. All this was entirely fictitious. He lectured for nearly an hour and impressed most of the audience, judging from a post-lecture evaluation. Many said in their comments that they would be interested to hear his lecture again because it had proved impossible to follow everything. Some even claimed to have read his research papers! Needless to say he hadn't written any!

If we consider the circumstances behind this experiment, we see just why Dr Fox 'foxed' his audience. First, he was given a big build-up: the person who introduced him informed the audience that he was an 'eminent expert in this valuable field of research'. We have seen from Chapter Two on attitudes how our expectations help shape the attention we pay to things. Here is a very good example of this. Secondly, Dr Fox had played the part of the serious lecturer very well: he made the right kind of gestures and above all he sounded authoritative, as though he knew what he was talking about. If we add the well-observed human trait that none of us likes to admit being a fool then you can see why this little experiment was so successful.

> **Consider any speakers who you have heard, live or on radio or TV, who impressed you by their presentation. What were the ingredients of their presentation which so attracted you?**

Naturally, what is dynamic to one person may not appear so to the next. However, there is enough research to suggest that it is the vocal qualities linked with certain non-verbal behaviours that give rise to most judgements of dynamism in presentation. The chief determining factor appears to be pace of presentation. There is evidence (Bowers, 1965) that speakers with a rapid pace are judged to be more clever and persuasive than slower speakers. There is obviously a point at which sheer pace gives way to incoherence, but we remember from our discussions on listening that one of the difficulties of effective listening was the slow speaker who encouraged his audience to daydream because of the discrepancy between the speed of speech and rapidity of a listener's thought processes. It is this sheer pace coupled with an intensity of projection and vitality – dynamism – that encourages our attention and often admiration. Sometimes, though, this very dynamism can be harnessed in ways which have profound consequences. Bullock (1968) writes of Hitler's oratory in the spring of 1938:

> As an orator Hitler had obvious faults. The timbre of his voice was harsh, very different from the beautiful quality of Goebbels's. He spoke at too great length; was often repetitive and verbose, lacked lucidity and frequently lost himself in cloudy phrases. These shortcomings mattered little beside the extraordinary impression of force, the immediacy of passion, the intensity of hatred, fury and menace conveyed by the sound of the voice alone without regard to what he said. (p. 373)

This example illustrates very well a most important point when it comes to any discussion on the topic of presenter credibility: that is the context in which any presentation takes place. We need to understand the setting, the influences and the general environment of speaker and audience. In the above example it is vital to appreciate the extent to which Hitler was addressing a people who felt ashamed and humiliated by an imposed peace after defeat in war. His oratory was designed to rouse his audience from humiliation to action, from despair to pride and from apathy to commitment – to the Nazi Party.

In assessing presenter credibility the boundaries imposed by time should be considered. In other words, how long do credible presenters remain so? You might like to consider which famous presenters – some mentioned above – will remain credible over time.

We have looked so far at some of the qualities that go up to make the effective and credible presentation. We have seen that such credibility is due to dynamic use of verbal and non-verbal techniques (eye contact, appropriate expression and gesture) and also to the way in which the material for the presentation is 'packaged' for the listener – its coherence and structure.

Persuasion

We saw from Bullock's description that Hitler was a persuasive speaker. Yet we also now know from the research – much of it in fact stimulated by the Second World War – that a great deal of what was believed to be obvious in terms of how persuasion occurs, turns out in fact to be anything but that.

Additional research has been stimulated by advertisers and campaign organizers anxious to discover whether their particular 'message' has got home or not. This is an enormous field in terms of communications research and literature. This section aims to give you an introduction and to suggest where you might go for further information.

The use of fear in a campaign has often been thought of as a powerful means of persuasion. The kind of campaign which warns us to stop smoking otherwise we will certainly die, or to stop eating sugar otherwise our teeth will fall out, has had a long history. There has been considerable evaluation of such campaigns (Soames, 1988); the view is now that the use of fear can in fact dull the impact of a campaign. The reason is that if people are frightened they will escape from the situation which is frightening them – the easiest way is to stop looking, or listening or reading. We have seen in our investigations of the theories of Cognitive Dissonance (Chapter Two, p. 26), that this kind of escape is very prevalent. This will help to explain why so many fear appeals have not been heeded. If the poster is showing something very painful for you, then why look?

One of the most famous studies into the use of fear appeals to influence people's behaviour was done by Janis & Flesbach (1953). They saw how young people would react to three different types of fear appeal: a very frightening warning about the dangers of tooth decay, a mild warning and a fainter one. They showed that it was the mild warning that was in fact the most heeded of the three. However, there are a number of reservations concerning this particular study. In the first place it has proved difficult to replicate; secondly, there were several rather special considerations behind the success of the mild appeal in their study. It was found that success depended on the provision of direct assistance to those whose interest had been aroused by the campaign. Where this was lacking – information as to clinics, treatment programmes, etc. – then even the mild fear campaign had little effect.

It does appear from a number of other studies (Janis & Terwilliger, 1962) that the use of high fear carrying appeals may well put off the receiver and cause the condition know as 'Reversed Effect'. In other words, recepients may shy away from the threat and ignore it because it is too nasty and unpleasant to contemplate. In the early 1960s there was a campaign to shock motorists into more careful driving. This was done by placing gruesome posters on the side of roads and at busy intersections. However, the results were disappointing. Motorists appear to have 'seen' the posters but shied away from taking the message in. Most health education appeals in recent years have moved away from the 'shock horror' type of attack towards more subtle campaigns. We saw from our examination of Cognitive Dissonance Theory (Chapter Two) that people when faced with this kind of hard-hitting information will rationalize and use all manner of ploys to escape the consequences of their actions.

There is increasing recognition that many variables will affect the success or failure of one particular appeal. We have seen with the AIDS campaigns that a variety of different messages have been aimed at the distinct groups thought to be at risk. One of the findings of earlier researchers such as Janis and Flesbach was that the success of a campaign depended upon the provision of direct access to professional help – in their case, dental services – as soon as any interest had been aroused. Where this kind of provision was lacking, such things as information as to clinics, treatment programmes, self-help groups, etc., then even mild fear campaigns had very little effect on the numbers coming foward for help or altering their behaviour.

> **Examine carefully, either in a group or on your own, a campaign such as that for AIDS which has had some measure of fear appeal built into it.**
>
> **Consider your, or your group's, reaction to it. Try to answer these questions: did it succeed in catching your interest? Did you feel like complying with the appeal? Did you feel like rejecting it? Why?**

Another aspect of research into the effect of persuasive appeals is the recognition that active audience participation is usually more effective in bringing about a change in attitude and behaviour than a campaign which is predominantly passive (Hovland, 1957).

It was in the Second World War that this effect began to be seriously examined. This was a time when, with the German U-boat menace cutting back supplies of traditional foodstuffs in the shops, the government had the job of persuading the population to eat 'new' foods such as stewed rhubarb with turnip pie. An investigation was carried out (Lewin, 1943) in which the same message was given to two different groups. In the first, nutritional experts gave information to an essentially passive audience. In the second, the audience were split up into groups, they discussed the advice given, debated the reasons for the government's campaign and asked questions of the speakers. The two groups were markedly different in their take-up of the nutritional advice. Those that had passively listened to the message with little or no participation were found to be mostly unmoved, while the second group who had had the opportunity to

discuss and actively participate were found to have a much higher
compliance rate with the campaign's aims.

**Consider why it was that this second group showed a much
higher rate of compliance. Jot down your answers. Have you
ever experienced this effect where you have been 'won over'
to a point of view not by being a passive listener but by
taking an active part in discussion?**

Persuaders have to take the nature and composition of groups very
seriously into account when aiming their material, since it is often
via the group that the message is attended to, filtered out,
discounted or reinforced: 'You don't want to take what they say', or
'Well, none of us have ever had that happen, so it can't be true'
(Taylor, 1978).

The third factor that is very apparent in the success of campaigns
which try to persuade us to change our behaviour or attitudes is the
technique of repetition. We don't have to be very alert to notice the
way in which advertisers make use of this device. No sooner had we
thought we had seen the last of one particular campaign when six
weeks later back it comes. It was one of the fundamental slogans of
the German Nazi Party that if one is to tell a lie 'make it a big one and
repeat it'.

Studies into brainwashing (Brown, 1978) indicate that the repetition of the same message, particularly where the subject is denied
access to other information, can have the effect of reducing resistance and the gradual acceptance of the message. It is interesting
that here the presence of group morale can be a decisive effect as
studies such as Brown's indicate from captured soldiers in the
Korean War. Where group morale was high, as with the Turkish
soldiers, many of them from the same village with a leader who was
one of them, then there was very little their Chinese brainwashers
could do. With many of the US forces, whose group moral was low
and officers remote, there was submission to the blandishments and
threats of their guards.

There is a risk in the constant repetition of slogans: this is the so-
called 'boomerang effect', where the constant hammering of a single
message causes people to become weary and hostile to it: 'Oh, no, not
this again'. The message then becomes a cliché and stale: this is the
problem with the no smoking campaigns. How does one keep a health
message before the public?

This explains why many advertising campaigns introduce slight
changes of style when repeated: there is then the familiarity of the
'old face' plus changes that may well prove intriguing and poten-
tially stimulating to the receiver. It also saves the campaign organizers a great deal of money by not having to totally re-make the
advert.

Mass Campaigns of Persuasion

We have already looked at the concept of credibility in terms of the single presenter faced with an audience. We can now enlarge this to the mass campaign produced for millions. The search for credibility is pursued remorselessly. This explains why we see pop stars selling fashion wear or chocolate bars or leading an anti-drugs crusade. The hope is that their credibility in one field, i.e., music, will rub off on to another. There is a risk here, since if some adverse publicity hits the star of the campaign then your campaign can be in trouble. This helps explain the fact that long-term credibility is a very precious commodity and a very precarious one: agents of media stars, for instance, take the greatest care not to allow this commodity to slip away through adverse publicity, gossip and scandal.

In our earlier definition of presenter credibility we saw how the use of statistics, examples, references, illustrations and topical accounts could enhance the status of the speaker in the eyes of the audience. The same is true when one considers mass campaigns of persuasion, such as the anti-Aids programme funded by the government. The use of statistics is considered to be helpful in 'packing' the message and making it more credible for its audience. However, there is a risk here: too many and vaguely put-about statistics may confuse or alienate the receiver. It is possible, thanks to the growing consumer movement that we are becoming more resistant to the abuse of statistics ('One in three of the population'; 'You have a 25 per cent chance of winning'). Backing general statements with topical and relevant examples can make a considerable difference to the credibility of a message (Kirkman & Turk, 1982). The crucial dimension here is relevance: that is something within the grasp and meaning of the receiver being aimed at (McQuail, 1972).

One aspect that has for long intrigued researchers into mass persuasion is whether it is best to give a one- or two-sided argument to your target audience. An opportunity presented itself at the close of the war in Europe in May 1945 for US researchers to undertake a quite massive study in this area. The problem was they had to decide which technique would be best to persuade US forces of the need to go on with the war against Japan. A one-sided message was tested out with one group of soldiers, while a two-sided approach was selected for another similarly matched group (Hovland & Lumsdane, 1949). What emerged from this study was that the one-sided approach was more effective with those soldiers who had had the least education, while the two-and-more-sided approach worked better with those with a college background. This study, which has been replicated a number of times, should not hold many surprises for us: presumably one of the aims of post-school education is to make people better at criticizing arguments. The findings certainly have implications for the managers of political parties and nationwide campaigns.

It is not just the question of one-sided versus multi-sided approaches that affect whether or not we 'buy' the message, nor is it entirely whether we see the message repeated or how credible the presenter of the message is; what also matters is whether we can accommodate the message. Bartlett's work (1932) into memory which we have already come across in Chapter Four on listening, suggested that in order to 'see' and remember messages it was necessary for them to be repeated in different forms. His work addressed itself to the need for managers not to rely on the oral channel for their communication but to use the written form as back-up wherever possible. We see this principle applied to many campaigns. First we may notice the poster displays, then later we see the same image on our TV screens, then find them appearing inside our daily and evening newspapers. We may also be aware of them as we walk by the shelves of our local supermarket and then find them plastered along the sides of the bus we take in the morning. We next may notice such signs on a friend's T-shirt or discreetly printed down his tie, on his golf clubs, her coffee mugs, record sleeves, ballpoint pen and inside the breakfast cereal packet as sponsor of a new approach to controlled dieting!

What does emerge from a study of the research literature on mass persuasion is the difficulty of 'hitting' all your audience with the one message. If, for example, we just take the UK as a mass audience we can see the difficulty of appealing equally to the Scots, Welsh, Ulster and English populations. This explains the rise of regional issues of newspapers, journals and magazines; the development of IBA local radio stations, cable networks and free newsheets. Alongside this development has come increasingly sophisticated means of discovering who the mass audience is for the particular campaign. Apart from the Registrar General's A, B, C1, C2, and D categories based on employment there are those like ACORN, based on house ownership. The increasing use of market surveys, shoppers' questionnaires, regional household buying trends etc., have added enormously to the intelligence that campaigners now have about us their target.

A popular recent development with advertising agencies has been the use of small group in-depth interviews. Here a representative sample of the target population is gathered together in a hotel and asked a number of structured questions about the product. They may be asked to view the advertisement or a first-draft mock-up. As well as recording their views, the observers working for the agency will be interested to view the non-verbal signals coming from their sample – for instance, their changes in facial expression, when shown the advertisement. This is an area where leakage is very closely monitored since there may well be a discrepancy between what is said and what is believed. A number of such groups will be gathered around the country so that as far as possible regional views are catered for.

Conclusions

The study of presentation skills is an enormous and expanding area. In the past perhaps too much time was spent on teaching people how to read and write their own language and not enough on the importance of being able to present ideas clearly and succintly in speech. Certainly school examinations in Britain until very recently have tended to dwell almost entirely on the written paper, only now are examination boards carrying out oral assessments. This has led to an increased interest in speech, but away from the old ideas of elocution, of speaking according to one particular accent or style and towards an approach more concerned with appropriacy of style and register. There has also been an renewed interest in how presentation skills can be taught, what kind of training best enables confidence to grow and skills to flourish.

In some areas, notably politics and the mass media, presentation has become a vital area of concern: reputations being made and broken, candidates selected or rejected because of their abilities at presenting themselves and their or others' ideas. Studies into rhetoric are now of more than passing interest to citizens in any democratic society.

Mass media campaigns also affect the lives of people in a modern society. The study of mass media in schools and colleges is perhaps one useful way in which to initiate future generations into the means and ways by which mass media operators make use of technique to achieve their effects. We have seen on occasions in this book that the simple equation so often given with regard to the popular media (e.g. TV violence equals a violent society), simply ignores the important and profound effects of attitude on the way in which we receive incoming messages, whether these are beamed at us from newsprint, satellite TV or poster displays in our city centres. This very fact has of course stimulated advertisers and campaign organizers to circumvent our 'natural' barriers. This has encouraged market research surveys, probe interviews to discover our hidden likes and dislikes, our prejudices and fears.

We hope that in this chapter and in the book we have provided you with starting points for your own discoveries of this area. We have tried to point out some of the main features in what is becoming a very crowded landscape. We hope you will have been tempted to explore for yourself.

Summary

1 Presentation to an audience works much better when there is maximum contact with that audience. This can be obtained when the speaker is looking up and not reading from notes, when the material is structured for easy assimilation, and pitched for the audience's

level of understanding, and when care is taken over the timing of the presentation.

2 Presenters, according to research into credibility, must be 'dynamic' – this involves using a variety of stimuli. Vocal monotony must at all costs be avoided. A variation of pace and tune together with appropriate eye contact helps to 'hold' an audience.

3 Presenters to mass audiences need to carefully prepare their material according to the 'needs' of that audience. This requires advance planning, surveys, questionnaires, etc. It is often better to aim for a smaller 'target' audience rather than trying to cover the whole population with the one message.

4 Fear appeals in persuasion must be handled carefully; it is all too easy to alarm an audience. The 'Law of Reversed Effort' comes into play here: the more you push your audience, the more they are likely to resist your advances. This has important implications for health education campaigns.

5 Campaigns of persuasion appear to be most successful when there is active participation by the audience rather than a delivery to a passive one. This active participation is best done in groups where there is plenty of opportunity to allow discussion and questions. Those who make up their own minds are much more likely to follow their own decisions.

6 Persuasion is helped when the presenters have high credibility with the audiences being addressed. Any such credibility may not last and care needs to be taken to ensure that the audience still has faith in the presenters selected; that their image is not tarnished or contaminated in some way so as to reduce their overall credibility.

7 The constant repetition of a message may enhance its persuasive impact. Care has to be taken to avoid the 'boomerang effect'; this is when boredom sets in. The repetition may be done in quite subtle ways: the message being slightly altered to puzzle the audience and thus keep them active and involved.

8 There is some risk that a many-sided message may not have the impact with less educated audiences that a simpler and more direct one would have. Here again the need for specific targeting of the audience is required. Care must be taken not to patronize an audience by aiming beneath their intelligence or awareness. This is particularly true with children and young people.

REFERENCES

AUSUBEL, D.P. (1976): *Educational psychology: a cognitive view.* Holt, Rinehart & Winston

BARTLETT, A. (1932): *Remembering*. Cambridge University Press

BOWERS, G. (1965): The influence of delivery on attitudes. *Speech Monographs* 32, 154–8

BROWN, A.C. (1978): *Techniques of persuasion*. Penguin

BROWN, G. (1982): *Learning from lectures*. University of Nottingham

BULLOCK, A. (1968): *Hitler, a study in tyranny*. Penguin

CHOMSKY, N. (1957): *Syntatic structures*. Cambridge, Massachussetts

DE SOTTO, C.B. (1960): Learning, a social structure. *Journal of Abnormal and Social Psychology* 60, 417–21

HOVLAND, C. (1957): *The order of presentation in persuasion*. Yale University Press

HOVLAND, C. & LUMSDANE, A. (1949): *Experiments on mass communication*. Princeton University Press

JANIS, I.L. & FLESBACH, S. (1953): Effects of fear arousing communications. *Journal of Abnormal and Social Psychology* 48, 78–92

JANIS, I.L. & TERWILLIGER, F. (1962): An experimental study of psychological resistance to fear-arousing communications. *Journal of Abnormal and Social Psychology*, 65, 493–501

KIRKMAN, J. & TURK, C. (1982): *Effective writing*. E. & F. Spon

LEWIN, D. (1943): The problems of changing food habits. *Bulletin of National Research Council Council*

LUND, F.H. (1929): The psychology of belief. *Journal of Abnormal and Social Psychology* 20, 183–91

McQUAIL, D. (1972): *Communication*. Longman

MORTENSEN, C.D. (1972): *Communication*. McGraw-Hill

NAFTULIN, D.H. & WARE, J.E. (1978): The Dr Fox syndrome: a paradigm of medical seduction. *Journal of Medical Education* 48, 15–16

NILES, C. (1963): Comprehension skills. *The Reading Teacher* 17, 2–7

NORTON, J. (1984): *Communicator style*. Sage

ORWELL, G. (1951): *1984*. Penguin

—— (1957): *Inside the whale and other essays*. Penguin

PATRICK, J. (1973): *A Glasgow gang observed*. Methuen

PASK, G. (1976): Styles and strategies of learning. *British Journal of Educational Psychology* 46, 128–48

REID, J. (1982): *A guide to effective study*. University of Edinburgh

ROSENSHINE, D. (1972): Enthusiastic teaching. In Holmes, J. (ed.), *The social psychology of teaching*. Penguin

SOAMES, R.F. (1988): Effective and ineffective use of fear in health promotion campaigns. *American Journal of Public Health* 78(2), 163–7

PACKHARD, V. (1982): *The hidden persuaders*. Penguin

INDEX